Crosscurrents / Modern Critiques / Third Series

Jerome Klinkowitz, General Editor

Also in this series:

Literary Subversions, by Jerome Klinkowitz

In Form: Digressions on the Act of Fiction, by Ronald Sukenick

Critical Angles: European Responses to Contemporary American Literature, edited by Marc Chénetier

The Theater of the American 1960s, by Zoltán Szilassy

Arthur M. Saltzman

The Fiction of William Gass
The Consolation of Language

Southern Illinois University Press
CARBONDALE AND EDWARDSVILLE

Copyright © 1986 by the Board of Trustees,
Southern Illinois University

Printed in the United States of America

Edited by Timothy S. Burns
Designed by Bob Nance
Production supervised by Kathleen Giencke

Library of Congress Cataloging in Publication Data
Saltzman, Arthur.
   The fiction of William Gass.
   (Crosscurrents/modern critiques. Third series)
   Bibliography: p.
   Includes index.
   1. Gass, William H., 1924–   —Criticism and interpretation.
I. Title.   II. Series.
PS3557.A845Z87   1985   813′.54   84-27714
ISBN 0-8093-1208-5

89 88 87 86 4 3 2 1

Dedicated to Marla and my parents
and to WHG—a fan's notes

Contents

Crosscurrents/
Modern Critiques/
Third Series

In the early 1960s, when the Crosscurrents/Modern Critiques series was developed by Harry T. Moore, the contemporary period was still a controversial one for scholarship. Even today the elusive sense of the present dares critics to rise above mere impressionism and to approach their subject with the same rigors of discipline expected in more traditional areas of study. As the first two series of Crosscurrents books demonstrated, critiquing contemporary culture often means that the writer must be historian, philosopher, sociologist, and bibliographer as well as literary critic, for in many cases these essential preliminary tasks are yet undone.

To the challenges that faced the initial Crosscurrents project have been added those unique to the past two decades: the disruption of conventional techniques by the great surge in innovative writing in the American 1960s just when social and political conditions were being radically transformed, the new worldwide interest in the Magic Realism of South American novelists, the startling experiments of textual and aural poetry from Europe, the emergence of Third World authors, the rising cause of feminism in life and literature, and, most dramatically, the introduction of Continental theory into the previously staid world of Anglo-American literary scholarship. These transformations demand that many traditional treatments be rethought, and part of the new responsibility for Crosscurrents will be to provide such studies.

Contributions to Crosscurrents/Modern Critiques/Third Series will be distinguished by their fresh approaches to established topics and by their opening up of new territories for discourse. When a single author is studied, we hope to present the first book on his or her work, or to explore a previously untreated aspect based on new research. Writers who have been critiqued well elsewhere will be studied in comparison with lesser-known figures, sometimes from other cultures, in an effort to broaden our base of understanding. Critical and theoretical works by leading novelists, poets, and dramatists will have a home in Crosscurrents/Modern Critiques/Third Series, as will sampler-introductions to the best in new Americanist criticism written abroad.

The excitement of contemporary studies is that all of its critical practitioners and most of their subjects are alive and working at the same time. One work influences another, bringing to the field a spirit of competition and cooperation that reaches an intensity rarely found in other disciplines. Above all, this third series of Crosscurrents/Modern Critiques will be collegial—a mutual interest in the present moment that can be shared by writer, subject, and reader alike.

Jerome Klinkowitz

Preface

Among contemporary American writers, William Gass stands out as a defender of the aesthetic integrity of fictional art. As both literary critic and fiction writer, Gass has produced some of the most elegant sentences to appear on the current cultural scene—an accomplishment very much in keeping with his theoretical belief that the artist is the maker of a verbal world whose value is not dependent upon its reference to the pre-existent world, but which is rather inherent and self-contained; consequently, the nature of textual reality is due to internal principles of coherence, rather than to its reflection of a pre-existent norm.

As such an argument would lead us to expect, Gass is regularly grouped with Barth, Barthelme, Hawkes, Nabokov, Pynchon, Sukenick, and other "metafictionists" who stress the fabric of their linguistic creations, and whose tendency is to place the physical properties of language and the overseeing presence of the author in the foreground of their works, thus calling attention to the process of imagination even as it is in operation. (Gass has declared that he is not principally

either a novelist or a critic, but a stylist, and that if asked to
write about his own work, "I would write about writing sentences.") Gass not only focuses upon the language that constitutes his scenes and characters, he luxuriates in it; no other
writer so unabashedly celebrates the sensual pleasures of
well-written words. His two honored essay collections, *Fiction
and the Figures of Life* and *The World Within the Word*, as well
as the protracted "philosophical inquiry," *On Being Blue*,
are dedicated to analyzing the ramifications of formal self-
reflection in literature, and to defining the moral, artistic,
and social implications of writing which disrupts and moves
beyond the conventions dictated by realistic fiction.

Surprisingly, Gass's fiction has not received the same attention accorded his criticism. This is strange because *Omensetter's Luck*, *Willie Masters' Lonesome Wife*, the stories in *In the
Heart of the Heart of the Country*, and the published fragments of
The Tunnel also consistently describe the tension between the
outside world, which is typically hostile, ambiguous, or just
blatantly uninspiring, and the world created by the shaping
energies of the artist. In each of these works, the artist's identity grows increasingly dependent upon the quality of the alternative world, or fiction, he devises for himself; moreover,
these comparatively hospitable, coherent structures come to
supersede any claims of "reality" upon the artist to the point
where private abstraction is his sole activity and comfort.

My investigation, therefore, concerns Gass's rigorous de-
mystification of the traditions of sequential plot, stable narration, verisimilitude, and the collaboration of the reader, who
is expected to suspend his disbelief in the artificiality of the
fiction that engages him; it equally concerns the consolation—for the reader, for Gass's obsessive characters, and for
the author himself—that self-evident, anti-illusionist art can
provide. Gass has often stated his firm belief that the essential

change that art can effect is a revolution of consciousness, and that ethical and aesthetic justifications of art are inseparable. Through his intricate, challenging fiction, Gass instructs and expands the appreciation of his readers. As he says in "The Artist and Society," works of art are important primarily "because they insist more than most on their own reality; because of the absolute way in which they exist."

I am indebted to the National Endowment for the Humanities for its financial assistance in the form of a summer stipend which enabled me to conduct my research. I also wish to acknowledge those journals in whose pages I was allowed to work out some of the themes of this book. Chapter Six, "The Aesthetics of Doubt in Recent Fiction," originally appeared, in slightly altered form, as an article in the Summer 1985 issue of *Denver Quarterly.* The argument that postrealist innovations in fictional form, contrary to charges of immorality or sheer self-indulgence, represent conscientious efforts to approach an ambiguous world with appropriate artistic strategies derives in large measure from William Gass's longstanding "debate" with John Gardner; using Gass's theoretical essays as my touchstone, I move outward to speak on recent American fiction in more general terms, proposing that works that question the mimetic basis of fiction may prove stylistically relevant to the views of reality which initiated them. The subsequent interview with William Gass, chapter 7 of this volume, was first published in the Summer 1984 issue of *Contemporary Literature,* and it serves to redirect these considerations of the nature of representation, language, and morality in art to focus on Gass's own writing career.

My thanks also goes to the publishers of Gass's works and to those resources from which I have chosen to quote at length for granting me permission to reprint significant passages. Finally, I want to thank William Gass for his continuing support and advice during the preparation of this project. His constructive responses, both in the form of personal interview and written commentary, were crucial influences upon the directions I have taken in the course of completing the book.

Acknowledgments

The following publishers have generously given permission to use extended quotations from copyrighted works:

From "Mimesis and the Motive for Fiction," by Robert Alter, in *TriQuarterly*, 42 (Spring 1978). Copyright © 1978 by *TriQuarterly*. Reprinted by permission of *TriQuarterly*, a publication of Northwestern University Press.

From *Watt*, by Samuel Beckett. Copyright © 1959 by Grove Press, Inc. Reprinted by permission of Grove Press, Inc.

From *Beautiful Theories: The Spectacle of Discourse in Contemporary Criticism*, by Elizabeth W. Bruss. Copyright © 1982 by The Johns Hopkins University Press, Inc. Reprinted by permission of The Johns Hopkins University Press, Inc.

From *The Book of Daniel*, by E. L. Doctorow. Copyright © 1971 by E. L. Doctorow. Reprinted by permission of Random House, Inc.

From *The Modern Century*, by Northrop Frye. Copyright © 1967 by Northrop Frye. Reprinted by permission of Oxford University Press.

From *Fiction and the Figures of Life,* by William H. Gass. Copyright © 1971 by William H. Gass. Reprinted by permission of the author.

From *In the Heart of the Heart of the Country,* by William H. Gass. Copyright © 1968 by William H. Gass. Reprinted by permission of Harper and Row, Inc.

From *Omensetter's Luck,* by William H. Gass. Copyright © 1966 by William H. Gass. Reprinted by permission of The New American Library, Inc.

From *On Being Blue: A Philosophical Inquiry,* by William H. Gass. Copyright © 1976 by William H. Gass. Reprinted by permission of David R. Godine, Publisher, Inc.

From *Willie Masters' Lonesome Wife,* by William H. Gass. Copyright © 1968 by William H. Gass. Reprinted by permission of *TriQuarterly,* a publication of Northwestern University Press.

From *The World Within the Word,* by William H. Gass. Copyright © 1978 by William H. Gass. Reprinted by permission of Alfred A. Knopf, Inc., and *Salmagundi.*

From *The Sense of an Ending: Studies in the Theory of Fiction,* by Frank Kermode. Copyright © 1977 by Oxford University Press. Reprinted by permission of Oxford University Press.

From *The Metafictional Muse: The Works of Robert Coover, Donald Barthelme, and William H. Gass,* by Larry McCaffery. Copyright © 1982 by University of Pittsburgh Press. Reprinted by permission of University of Pittsburgh Press.

From "An Interview with William Gass," conducted by Bradford Morrow, in *Conjunctions,* 4 (Spring-Summer 1983). Copyright © 1983 by *Conjunctions.* Reprinted by permission of *Conjunctions.*

From *The Dehumanization of Art and Other Essays on Art, Culture and Literature,* by José Ortega y Gasset, trans. Helen Weyl.

Copyright © 1948, 1968 by Princeton University Press. Reprinted by permission of Princeton University Press.

From *From Baudelaire to Surrealism,* by Marcel Raymond, trans. G. M. Copyright © 1949 by Wittenborn Art Books, Inc. Reprinted by permission of Wittenborn Art Books, Inc.

From "Individual Voice in the Collective Discourse: Literary Innovation in Postmodern American Fiction," by Charles Russell, in *Sub-stance,* 27 (1980). Copyright © 1980 by The University of Wisconsin Press. Reprinted by permission of The University of Wisconsin Press.

From "Donald Barthelme, William Gass, Grace Paley, Walker Percy: A Symposium on Fiction," *Shenandoah,* 27 (Winter 1976). Copyright © 1976 by Washington and Lee University. Reprinted by permission of the Editor of *Shenandoah: The Washington and Lee University Review.*

From *Four in America,* by Gertrude Stein. Copyright © 1947 by Yale University Press. Reprinted by permission of Yale University Press.

From *Language and Silence: Essays on Language, Literature, and the Inhuman,* by George Steiner. Copyright © 1963, 1967, 1976 by George Steiner. Reprinted by permission of Atheneum Publishers.

From *The Death of the Novel and Other Stories,* by Ronald Sukenick. Copyright © 1969 by Ronald Sukenick. Reprinted by permission of Ronald Sukenick and ICM.

From "Thirteen Digressions," by Ronald Sukenick, in *Partisan Review,* 43, no. 1 (1976). Copyright © 1976 by *Partisan Review.* Reprinted by permission of *Partisan Review* and Ronald Sukenick.

From "Twelve Digressions Toward a Study of Composition," by Ronald Sukenick, in *New Literary History,* 6 (1975). Copyright © 1975 by The Johns Hopkins University Press. Reprinted by permission of The Johns Hopkins University Press.

From "Introduction to the Series," by Lee Thayer, in *The Broken Word: The Communication Pathos in Modern Literature,* by Winston Weathers. Copyright © 1981 by Gordon and Breach, Inc. Reprinted by permission of Gordon and Breach, Inc.

From *War and Peace,* by Leo Tolstoy, in the Norton Critical Edition edited by George Gibian (1966), trans. Louise and Aylmer Maude. Copyright © 1933 by Oxford University Press. Reprinted by permission of Oxford University Press.

From *Slaughterhouse-Five, or The Children's Crusade,* by Kurt Vonnegut, Jr. Copyright © 1969 by Kurt Vonnegut, Jr. Reprinted by permission of Delacorte Press/Seymour Lawrence.

The Fiction of William Gass
The Consolation of Language

Like the spirit of a plant or an animal, it has an architecture of its own, and adorns nature with a new thing.

Ralph Waldo Emerson, "The Poet"

What constitutes the novelist's strength is precisely that he invents, that he invents quite freely, without a model. The remarkable thing about modern fiction is that it asserts this characteristic quite deliberately, to such a degree that invention and imagination become, at the limit, the very subject of the book.

Alain Robbe-Grillet,
"On Several Obsolete Notions"

All writing, all composition, is construction. We do not imitate the world, we construct versions of it. There is no mimesis, only poesis. No recording, only constructing.

Robert Scholes,
"The Fictional Criticism of the Future"

1

Introduction: Wording a World

ONE OF THE HALLMARKS of contemporary post-realist American fiction (aside from the abundance of unwieldy terms like this) is the pleasure it takes in its own form. When reading Barth, Barthelme, Coover, Federman, Pynchon, Sorrentino, Sukenick, and other writers usually mentioned with them, we are perhaps struck by nothing more profoundly than the sheer energy of invention that their writing exhibits. Lyrical flights and structural ingenuity combine to stretch the conventional boundaries of fiction, so much so that the very concept of stable convention has been disrupted beyond repair.[1]

William Gass is notable among these writers both as a particularly intrepid explorer into the frontiers of fictional style and as a theoretical proponent of postrealism. Few writers, not even those who may appear more rigorously experimental or technically extravagant, so effectively promote an appreciation of the language object for its own splendid sake; few devote such rigorous attention to the sensual properties of words:

but I have been dropping hints all along like heavy shoes . . . that the true sexuality in literature—sex as a positive aesthetic quality—lies not in any scene and subject, nor in the mere appearance of a vulgar word, not in the thick smear of a blue spot, but in the consequences on the page of love well made—made to the medium which is the writer's own, for he—for she—has only these little shapes and sounds to work with, the same saliva surrounds them all, every word is equally a squiggle or a noise, an abstract designation (the class of cocks, for instance, or the sub-class of father-defilers), and a crowd of meanings as randomly connected by time and use as a child connects his tinkertoys. On this basis, not a single thing will distinguish 'fuck' from 'fraise du bois'; 'blue' and 'triangle' are equally abstract; and what counts is not what lascivious sights your loins can tie to your thoughts like Lucky is to Pozzo, but love lavished on speech of any kind, regardless of content and intention.[2]

Gass's well-publicized "erotics" of language is tempered by a contemporary postrealist sensibility which demystifies both artist and artifact. We are by now accustomed to the major characteristics of that sensibility: overt artificiality and self-consciousness regarding the creative act; playfulness of tone and formal virtuosity, whose dazzle often results from a sense of tightrope-walking over the void; and possibly most evident of all, a ruthless skepticism toward verisimilitude, which had once served as the goal and standard of the realist program, and against which the writings of the aforementioned authors constitute an elaborate reaction. As Gass himself wonders, "has not the world become, for many novelists, a place not only vacant of gods, but also empty of a generously regular and peacefully abiding nature on which the novelist might, in large, rely, so to concentrate on cutting a fine and sculptured line through a large mass taken for granted . . . so that, with all these forms of vacantness about him, he has felt the need to reconstitute, entire, his world?"[3]

In order to understand the significance of these questions for Gass, for experimental fiction, and for the process of understanding fiction as a whole, we must begin by investigating the breakdown of systems for uncovering and displaying meaning, among which novels have traditionally been consequential examples, and how that breakdown reflects a situation upon which so many contemporary writers have come to agree: the illusory, or nightmarish, nature of reality.

As it does in our extra-literary lives, the erosion of certainty in contemporary fiction seems to continue unabated; nevertheless, testifying to our capacity either for resilience or resignation, contemporary fiction and its attending criticism have grown increasingly casual about the indeterminacy of our world. Some rather disturbing issues—the arbitrariness of values, the ambiguity of purpose, the relativity of meaning—are now described by such common terms as the Absurd and Black Humor. In short, the world of experience (for by now, "real world" lodges like something mis-swallowed) suffers regular discredit; those who find it chaotic and hostile balk at its authority, while those who find it incomprehensible complain that it provides no reliable foundation for belief or action. Ronald Sukenick's description of the systematic demise of "givens" upon which fiction had once rested is representative:

The contemporary writer—the writer who is acutely in touch with the life of which he is part—is forced to start from scratch: Reality doesn't exist, time doesn't exist, personality doesn't exist. God was the omniscient author, but he died; now no one knows the plot, and since our reality lacks the sanction of a creator, there's no guarantee as to the authenticity of the received version. Time is reduced to presence, the content of a series of discontinuous moments. Time is no longer purposive, and so there is no density, only chance. Reality is, simply, our experience, and objectivity is, of course, an illusion. Personality, after passing through a stage of awkward self-consciousness, has become, quite minimally, a mere locus for our experience. In view of these annihilations, it should be no surprise that literature, also, does not exist—how could it? There is only reading and writing, which are things we do, like eating and making love, to pass the time, ways of maintaining a considered boredom in face of the abyss.

Not to mention a series of overwhelming social dislocations.[4]

Sukenick's is mock distress, for although realistic fiction may have been forced to examine its tenets, it continues vigorously on. The effect of this redefinition upon recent American fiction has been a de-emphasis on mimetic accuracy. In a sense, writers have countered rejection with indifference: since the world is stubbornly immune to interpretation, fiction responds by locating meaning internally. Thus, the writer demonstrates his abilities where they produce tangible results—in the arena of language. If the world refuses to provide inherent significance, the artist must take up the burden by constructing significance provisionally.

This is, after all, an understandable response to the loss of faith in man's ability to know. Heady optimism about our objective powers of observation found its artistic counterpart in literary realism; however, a loss of that confidence demands a style of writing, as well as an attitude toward the creative act, that is appropriate to indeterminacy—realistic not in the sense of literary realism, but in the sense of fidelity to postrealist conception of man's diminished authority in a relativistic, stupefying universe. As Iris Murdoch points out, "Since reality is incomplete, art must not be too afraid of incompleteness."[5]

Reality deflects the traditional aims of rationality. Fragmentary and alien—a chaos beyond words—reality brings us to a crisis of intelligibility, which has been generally accepted by modern art as commonplace:

This world is dense, opaque, unintelligible; that is the datum from which the modern artist always starts. The formal dictates of the well-made play or the well-made novel, which were the logical outcome of thoroughly rational preconceptions about reality, we can no longer hold to when we become attentive "to the things themselves," to the facts, to existence in the mode in which we do exist. If our epoch still held to the idea, as Western man once did, that the whole of reality is a system in which each detail providentially and rationally is subordinated to others and ultimately to the whole itself, we could demand of the artist that his form imitate this idea of reality, and give us coherence, logic, and the picture of a world with no loose ends. But to make such a demand nowadays is worse than an impertinence: it is a travesty upon the historical being of the artist.[6]

Recent experiments in fictional form suggest that mimesis not only is outmoded, but that, because of our inevitable distance from the world, it was never an attainable goal. One of the corrupting effects upon that doctrine is the tendency to anthropomorphize the world. This tendency is hardly surprising. By upholstering the world with our own preoccupations and associations, we make it less mysterious, more accessible. Like Thomas Pynchon's Fausto Maijstral, the enigmatic diarist in *V.*, we recoil from the vision of the essential nonhumanity of reality: "Fausto's kind are alone with the task of living in a universe of things which simply are, and cloaking that innate mindlessness with comfortable and pious metaphor."[7] Our reluctance to purify the world of humans stems from this need to accommodate it comfortably. We are reminded of Samuel Beckett's Watt, whose concerted efforts to penetrate the aloofness of his surroundings are consistently frustrated; even the most mundane objects resist his understanding: "Looking at a pot, for example, or thinking of a pot, at one of Mr. Knott's pots, it was in vain that Watt said Pot, pot. Well, perhaps not quite in vain, but very nearly. For it was not a pot, the more he looked, the more he reflected, the more he felt sure of that, that it was not a pot at all. It resembled a pot, it was almost a pot, but it was not a pot of which one could say, Pot, pot, and be comforted."[8] As Beckett's hero demonstrates, the only fixity we can honestly discover is the "fixity of mystery."[9]

Because our automatic recourse is to project pre-existent emotions and meanings upon the world, so that what then appears to us as truth is principally a reflection of our own subjective distortions, every observation we make is an interpretation. Werner Heisenberg submits that this is true in the sciences as well; his "Uncertainty Principle" states that the act of observation intrudes upon and alters the events being observed; "Natural science does not simply explain and describe nature; it describes nature as exposed to our method of questioning."[10] In other words, by denying objects and events their integrity in order to make them comprehensible—available to some system of inquiry, or some fictional order with which we are already familiar—we regularly misrepresent the fact "that things are here and that they are nothing but things, each limited to itself."[11]

When we try to come to terms with the world, therefore, we must do so through a medium—specifically, language—which again filters and adulterates perception. This interfering filter is what Frank Kermode calls the "irreducible minimum of geometry," the basic human need for structure, which enters in the form of fiction between man and an unprotected confrontation with reality.[12] In *Willie Masters' Lonesome Wife,* Gass states, "No one can imagine simply—merely; one must imagine within words or paint or metal, communi-

cating genes or multiplying numbers. Imagination is its medium realized."[13] Words are an especially troublesome medium because, in contrast to pigment or numbers, they carry
previously defined meanings. Because they already name
things and are contaminated by their attachments in the
world, their usefulness as tools for objectively comprehend-
ing the world is severely compromised.

Our daily apprehension of the world is refracted by a complex system of preconceived attitudes and connotations
which accompanies our language. José Ortega y Gasset, in
his well-known metaphor of the window and the garden, argues that any insistence that we are perceiving without im-
pediment implies an automatic optical adjustment that ignores the interference of the language system: "But not many
people are capable of adjusting their perceptive apparatus to
the pane and the transparency that is the work of art. Instead
they look right through it and revel in the human reality with
which the work deals. When they are invited to let go of this
prey and to direct their attention to the work of art itself they
will say they cannot see such a thing, which indeed they cannot, because it is all artistic transparency and without sub-
stance."[14] He goes on to defend a brand of art which requires
aesthetic appreciation above and beyond sentimental identification with its plotted "human content." Because the window, which is identified as the artwork or fiction through
which we perceive, is transparent, it is difficult to recognize
its mediating effect.

William Gass is even more uncompromising in his suspicion of language as a means for establishing contact with the
world. His argument is that words are not glass but stone, not
transparent but opaque, and thus even less amenable to the
mission of conveying external reality to the reader. Gass provides an alternative metaphor for the manner in which lan-

guage operates in fiction, one which sees the relationship between sign and referent as far more elusive than does
Ortega's, and he confounds literary realism's claim of concrete detection: "On the other side of a novel lies the void.
Think for instance, of a striding statue; imagine the purposeful inclination of the torso, the alert and penetrating gaze of
the head and its eyes, the outstretched arm and pointing finger; everything would appear to direct us toward some goal
in front of it. Yet our eye travels only to the finger's end, and
not beyond. Though pointing, the finger bids us stay instead,
and we journey slowly back along the tension of the arm. In
our hearts we know what actually surrounds the statue. The
same surrounds every other work of art: empty space and silence."[15]

What results from this radical reassessment of fiction is a
repudiation of the dictates of an external reality whose avail-
ability was never trustworthy anyway. A severely qualified,
heavily self-conscious co-existence is established between the
self and its surroundings. Gass concedes throughout his writing the elusiveness of what hovers just beyond the fiction one
creates; he does this the most memorably in "In the Heart of
the Heart of the Country," whose introverted narrator confesses, "We meet on this window, the world and I, inelegantly,
swimmers of the glass; and swung wrong way round to one
another, the world seems in."[16]

The fact that the world we inhabit denies our attempts to
contact it is potentially a source of despair and stagnation;
however, as evidenced by the outpouring of postrealist fiction, it rouses our creative resources. The world, or at least a
world, is ours to invest with meaning and stability. Indeed,
the experimental fictionist provocatively reasons, because all
systems and perspectives are inescapably subjective—and this
is to say synthetic—one can invent with impunity. Mimesis,
if that term is still pertinent, turns inward: what is imitated is

consciousness itself. Whether or not this private realm provides a feeling for some universal, external coherence, is problemmatical at best. According to John Ditsky, one of the hallmarks of recent innovative fiction is the assumption "that the 'real' world is only surface appearances, acquiring meaning only when humans invest them with it. Therefore, no attempt to observe the 'rules' of time and space in the apparent world can be expected; one moves in and out of formerly rigidly barricaded planes of existence, an eclecticism of motion that is the stuff of dreaming."[17] The "reality" of the artwork resides in the integrity of its form, not in the accuracy of its depiction of what lies outside it. Alain Robbe-Grillet, whose *For a New Novel* is something of an early manifesto for postrealist fiction, insists on the obsolescence of any standard of judgment which restricts the writer's freedom to invent new works and new means of evaluating these works: "The existence of a work of art, its weight, are not at the mercy of interpretive grids which may or may not coincide with its contours. The work of art, like the world, is a living form: it *is,* it has no need of justification."[18] Forsaking a descriptive function, the novel asserts itself as a competing reality, a new object to be contended with—in Gass's words, a world of words.

After being liberated from these disqualified expectations, the literary artist wins an exalted status, for he is supplementing reality as opposed to merely viewing it. The verbal system which results is both imaginative and concrete. Ronald Sukenick, a principal apostle of this revolutionary attitude, applauds this escape from the constraints of literary realism as a way of renewing our faith in the unlimited resourcefulness of the imagination: "Rather than serving as a mirror or redoubling on itself, fiction adds itself to the world, creating a meaningful 'reality' that did not previously exist. Fiction is artifice but not artificial. It seems as pointless to call the creative powers of the mind 'fraudulent' as it would to call the procreative powers of the body such."[19] Therefore, meaning is also "created" through verbalization instead of being reproduced from life.

The autonomy of the work of fiction, then, extends beyond its style to include its significance as well, and it is at this point that some readers whose moorings are in the familiar harbor of realism become unsettled. "It seems a country-headed thing to say: that literature is language, that stories and the places and the people in them are merely made of words as chairs are made of smoothed sticks and sometimes of cloth or metal tubes," muses William Gass in "The Medium of Fiction." "That novels should be made of words, and merely words, is shocking, really. It's as though you had discovered that your wife were made of rubber: the bliss of all those years, the fears . . . from sponge."[20] But of course, surgery on one's wife would be no less disconcerting: the discovery of arteries and organs, like that of the words which make up a beloved text, is simply the adjustment of focus of which Ortega speaks, and yet, suddenly one is made aware of how fragile the surface of familiarity can be.

To be sure, as Gass argues, the very notion of character is so utterly dismantled by this reconsideration of conventional ideas that literary characters are, in essence, robbed of their "human dimension." Because all elements in a fictional context are language, and then, when they are read and digested by the mind, contents of consciousness, all components of that context must be recognized as "characters." All are linguistic components of a given text; mountains, rivers, images, repeated phrases, are all characters, all instances of ordered language. Gass's formula is most democratic: "Characters are those primary substances to which everything else is attached."[21] This is a disturbing concept for anyone who has ever sighed for Emma Bovary or cringed before

Captain Ahab: characters are essentially wordstuff, textual placeholders, and remembered sound.

Gass goes on to support the primacy of words as objects by explaining that they serve a different purpose in an artistic context than they do in daily speech. Whereas "Hello," "Stop," and "Pass the butter" are disposable commodities when used in daily speech, brought into being only to vanish immediately after their function of designation is accomplished, words in a literary work are meant to be lingered over and lovingly tongued. They are permanent fixtures in the world. We are reminded of Borges' story, "Tlön, Uqbar, Orbis Tertius," in which certain meticulously imagined objects (called "hrönir") have the capacity to become actual, taking their place and asserting their authority and authenticity in the world. Gass makes the point that fiction always aspires to the status of being an addition to reality. Because his contribution is so consequential, the artist need never apologize for the creation of fictions as a means of influencing reality: "Very frequently the writer's aim is to take apart the world where you have very little control, and replace it with language over which you can have some control."[22] Thus, when T. S. Eliot speaks of the fragments he shores against his ruins in the closing lines of *The Waste Land,* he is referring not only to the process of intellection he has just completed but also to the selection and arrangement of words in the poem itself: they comprise a world more hospitable to the artist's needs and more amenable to his manipulation. This is the source of the artist's consolation for the insufficiency of the modern world.

The language of fiction is valuable for its own aesthetic sake, not merely, nor even primarily, for its ability to summon any reality outside itself. In fact, based upon the argument that coherence is the chief factor in evaluating fiction,

Gass proposes that the artist's mission is not to prescribe an adequate philosophy to be employed by his readers, but rather to create a philosophically adequate system, whose legitimacy is measured by its internal consistency instead of by its adaptability to the modern world—the disdain of which initiates the verbal alternative in the first place.[23] We can extend this thought by saying that the artist replicates nature's own activities; he appropriates its processes and competes on the terms it dictates. Vladimir Nabokov echoes Gass in claiming separate and equal existence for the work of art: "To call a story a true story is an insult both to art and truth. Every great writer is a great deceiver, but so is that arch-cheat Nature. Nature always deceives. . . . The writer of fiction only follows Nature's lead."[24]

Ideally, the world of words provides an environment far more receptive to the structuring talents of the composer, and if only for that reason, it can become a seductive refuge from a world which is hostile to composition. (How poor a currency are words, but how rich a treasure!) So begins the justification of retreat presented by Gass's "heroes of language." Having failed to transform reality with art, they turn to the rewards which art does offer: a bastion of meaning and the security of verbal insulation. "I live *in,*" announces the narrator of "In the Heart of the Heart of the Country," with no small satisfaction.[25] If language cannot capture and subdue the world, perhaps it can keep it at bay by supplanting it with some aesthetic substitute.

In this view of the verbal world, in which "there are no events but words,"[26] words are granted a "first-order" reality that exceeds a purely referential importance. In contrast to the outside world, where details, dialogues, and activities accumulate without apparent motive or connection, the world within sets forth ulterior significance. Gass declares that the well-made novel (he uses Malcolm Lowry's *Under the Volcano* as an example) is a "net of essential relations" whose capacity for offering and ensuring meaning easily surpasses the haphazard reality surrounding its conception: "Nothing like history, then, the *Volcano* ties time in knots, is utterly subjective, completely contrived, as planned and patterned as a magical rug where the figure becomes the carpet."[27] The novelist's creation aspires to a self-contained referential system. Furthermore, the experience of the world of words holds up quite well against other life experiences; because it is specifically constructed to foster significant experience, this artificial world actually proves to be more substantial than other "real," but less calculated, experiences. As Gass proclaims, language is "more powerful as an experience of things than the experience of things. Signs are more potent experiences than anything else, so when one is dealing with the things that really count, then you deal with words. They have a reality far exceeding the things they name . . . the very experience of symbols is now the important experience. . . . In the old days we might have supposed that the daffodil was much, much more interesting than the word daffodil, but I simply would deny that. The word daffodil is much more interesting than daffodils. There's much more to it."[28]

For art to function in this exalted manner, it must result from efforts equally as strenuous as those required by life itself. Surely the motivations behind it are as serious: "One's complete sentences," says Gass, "are attempts, as often as not, to complete an incomplete self with words."[29] Once thought to be an instrument of approaching the outside world, the novel is hereby shown to be appreciated for its own well-wrought reality, and the outside world stands betrayed by the novel's insistence on its own formal being.

So formidable a transformation of the roles of art and artist, however, disturbs more than just the reader's conventional manner of responding to fiction; it also jeopardizes the stability of the "construction" itself. To argue that the work of art does not correspond in any essential way to the outside world is to contaminate the order it proposes, since its autonomy renders that order merely provisional. The act of attempting to compensate for the failures of religion, science, philosophy, and social institutions to serve us dependably is in itself an indictment of the lack of authority behind that effort. In short, as Gerald Graff reasons in *Literature Against Itself,* the mere belief or statement that art endows the world, or a world, with meaning, manifests the arbitrary nature of that meaning. Moreover, whatever significance is ascribed to art in order to justify its universality must be eliminated to guarantee its innocence and authenticity—high priorities for the contemporary fiction writer who seeks to compose a self-contained verbal reality.[30] Seen from this viewpoint, art succumbs to the same doubts and relativism that have affected other systems: the innovative novel is as symptomatic of the disrupted state of affairs in today's world as are any of the other disqualified systems for which it hopes to substitute. Since the novel is instigated with an attitude of skepticism and scorn toward the outside world, we can hardly expect absolute faith in any system, even a private, self-imposed one, to be easily sustained.

The artist's admission that his vision is subjective, that it does not confront external reality, and that its foremost aim is to advance itself and not to explicate some overriding Truth "out there" ironically undercuts the "nobility" of his commitment. "Could not one say," Graff asks, "that the artist who saves himself by inventing fictions of order he knows to be arbitrary is engaging in a deception of which the confused observer is innocent?"[31] The ground rules for his game expose it as counterfeit, and thus diminish its usefulness and appeal.

If the attempt to leave the world behind is one problem with which the postrealist writer must contend, the possibility that the escape is illusory is another. As discussed earlier, language is the artistic medium most charged with mediacy; because it is appropriated from the world, its use in an artistic context still conjures that world to some extent. Weighted down by preconceptions, "the writer's medium differs from the media of most other arts—pigment, stone, musical notes, etc.—in that it is never virgin: words come to the writer already violated by other men, impressed with meanings derived from the world of common experience. Thus, there is always a natural temptation to regard the writer as a man who tells us something, rather than as a man who tells us something by making something."[32] Equating construction with contention does a disservice to the verbal artifact. Gass argues that the use of language in fiction only imitates its use in daily life, where it earns only fleeting notice anyway; in fiction, however, the sign is there to be dwelled upon, or even, as in the case of Gass's own richly textured, heavily metaphorical prose, luxuriated in. Words are ontologically transformed by their inclusion in a novel in much the same way as a carrot is transformed by its inclusion in a snowman's face; this means that the nature of being is a matter of context.[33] We can compare this to Magritte's faithfully realistic painting of a pipe, entitled "The Treason of Images," whose caption (translated as "This is not a pipe") bids us remember that "every successful work supersedes its model and renders the world superfluous to it."[34]

Between these extreme views on the relationship between the two worlds is the uncomfortable middle ground, which is that language in fiction occupies the no-man's land between signification and pure self-referential significance. As Alan Wilde reminds us, the artwork cannot entirely conceal its indebtedness to that indomitable "parent reality," and the intricacy of the deftly patterned text ironically confesses itself as the product of premeditation beyond its boundaries—a creative concept which it inevitably answers to: "But however fantasticated, the world is there: an undeniable pressure exerting itself against the story's reflexiveness."[35] In the best postrealist fiction, this is a dynamic antagonism that is both thematically and stylistically prominent, but once again, the fact that the external world is by no means eradicated by the completion of the verbal world limits the self-sufficiency of the text. Of interest here are the terms "centrifugal" and "centripetal," used by Northrop Frye to describe the tension inherent in the reading process. We simultaneously move outward from the words on the page to their conventional meanings and associations, and inward to a closer contemplation of the verbal pattern itself. Frye does point out, corroborating Gass, that the conclusive direction of meaning is centripetal, but the influence of centrifugal claims to our attention, though it may be subordinated, is not eliminated.[36]

Another potential pitfall of the art which Richard Poirier describes as "furiously self-consultive"[37] is shown in the fates of those characters who practice it. In Gass's novels, characters who maneuver themselves into vaults of language tend to suffocate from the rarefied atmosphere. Indeed, to suggest that the retreat into language is merely a strategy, a chosen opportunity to rejuvenate one's waning forces in preparation for a vigorous return to reality, is to ignore how very consistently Gass's wordmongers find the retreat to be an end in itself, and prove either unwilling or incapable of moving beyond its confinement. We discover throughout the fiction an insidious degeneration from sanctuary into prison. Reverend Jethro Furber, in *Omensetter's Luck,* withdraws into a surrogate Eden whose boundaries are garden walls and overgrown rhetoric; he resultantly finds himself haunted by his isolation and the despicable company of his own thoughts. Jorge, faced with uncompromising surroundings in "The Pedersen Kid," numbly endures a blizzard in the Pedersens' basement, where he fosters a warm privacy apart from the shocking facts of the story; the narrator of "Mrs. Mean" is overawed by his subject partly as a result of having fantasticated her because he is not able to confront her more directly than from the shadows; Fender, in "Icicles," removes himself into narcissistic dreams which, like the ruling image of the story, become a static trap; the frustrated housewife who narrates "The Order of Insects" escapes from the disorder and drabness of her life by developing a fascination for the physical intricacy of bugs, but theirs is the quiet beauty of death; the narrator of "In the Heart of the Heart of the Country" suffers from a psychological climate as barren and unremittingly hopeless as his physical surroundings; and Babs, the title figure of *Willie Masters' Lonesome Wife,* seeks in words a warmer embrace than any man would provide but finds that she only intensifies her loneliness and is reduced to "a string of noises." All are monologists, all are reluctant to surrender the sense of rhythm and control that an alienated, uninterrupted voice affords.[38] While it is true that their artificial alternatives offer many of the consolations of art—beauty, permanence, organization, value—we never forget that they come at a high price, because fulfillment and vitality are sacrificed in the bargain.

Fictions do not lead to a transcendence of fictional requirements as readily as they plunge their practitioners deeper into abstraction; once rejected, tenancy in the outside world cannot easily be restored. The wicked irony is that escape may just be estrangement in disguise, and that the feelings of loss and exile which beleaguer Gass's characters are often a

dubious alternative to the anxieties which precipitated the repudiation of "public life."

Still another disadvantage of the verbal realm is that characters lose their contours when they are steeped in the lush
jungles of language. All but voice is obscured. Gass's prose
style is strikingly rich; it is thick with alliteration, allusion,
parallel patterns, imagery, assonance, and strong rhythms.
When they are waylaid from the world and then submerged
into a language like this, characters who might thrive in a
more traditionally realistic story dissolve like sugar cubes.
Recall that Gass poses the analogy of the transubstantiation
of an object when it is removed from its usual context and
planted in an alien one—the disquisition of the snowman's
nose—to explain how words undergo an ontological change
when they are taken from everyday speech and employed in
fiction; so, too, are worldly possessions and personalities
changed. In fact, in the case of Gass's narrators, it might be
more accurate to compare them to carrots dropped into a
snowdrift: the new context overwhelms them.

Nevertheless, at least in the narrators' estimation, the
threat posed by the environment of language pales before
that posed by an ambiguous, inimical external reality; if their
choice is to be between coherent parsimony and chaotic
abundance, Gass's leading characters regularly opt for the
former. Coherence takes precedence over other criteria for
judging a system; although an invented system is assailable
on the grounds of restrictiveness and arbitrariness, thus rendering the consolation of language tentative, external reality
is by no means free of the same drawbacks. Demeaning a fictional alternative for being a hollow parody assumes that it
can be compared to some authentic or non-degraded form—
a universally agreed-upon reality—whereas the lesson of the
preponderance of postrealist fiction is that no such objective

system exists. ("Words lie only to those who are haunted by
the truth of words," cautions Raymond Federman in *The
Twofold Vibration*).[39] This revelation can be bracing, however,
because it offers the diligent artist the chance to fabricate as
elegant and ruthlessly patterned a private world as he is able
to conceive. The trouble arises among those agitated artists
who feel compelled to expand their idiosyncratic realities,
any one of which is insufficient in itself, into Reality. This
necessarily denies the fullness of experience, and as kings of
nutshells, these artists spend their time buttressing their fictions with endless justifications: "I lie in the crack of a book
for my comfort . . . it's what the world offers . . . please leave
me alone to dream as I fancy," mutters Jethro Furber, for
whom language has become a disease.[40]

By contrast, Gass himself takes more satisfactory advantage of the freedom to invent by advancing his art without re-
sorting to self-delusion about the world's existence. He contends that not only is all literature experience, but all
experience is literary: all experience, whether lived, read, or
otherwise engaged in, is digested as narrative.[41] In other
words, perception distills everything into mental structures;
in this form the secular and the textual are equally value-
laden and equally "real." Language is the conferrer of stature; its power is best realized when we remember Gass's repeated pronouncements regarding the physical presence and
tangible rewards of words. Gass avoids the solipsistic impasse
faced by his fictional artists because, for him, pattern and
sound are architectural triumphs which he leads us through
as though they were mansions. Above all, Gass is a hospitable writer, not in the sense of writing simple stories, but in the
sense of being eager to construct objects which are "worthy of
love."[42] Unlike his generally misanthropic narrators, Gass
invites us in.

Under Gass's scrupulous supervision, language aspires to the state of heroic enterprise. Naomi Lebowitz suggests that this will be a chief direction in the growth of the modern novel: "The old character, morality, and metaphysics are mere shadows with which substantially fleshed words can box. The maker of metaphors is . . . master of infinite disguises, and this lying . . . is meant to deceive us into the one truth—that fiction is a holy compensation for the loss of consoling gods. The novelist as hero uses his words to parody social relationships or spiritual yearnings, not as much in scorn of moral or metaphysical seriousness as in protest against aesthetic limitations."[43] Language, when used as a refuge of artistic sanctity, confirms one's distance from the vulgar and the mundane; protection of and in the mind reflects a desire to improve upon the available world, which does not accommodate spiritual projects so effectively as do verbal enclaves.

What is so intriguing about Gass's work is its exploration of the tension between the desire to create seamless, autotelic worlds and the responsibility to direct our attention to what Gilbert Sorrentino calls "the imaginative qualities of actual things,"[44] which is to say, to the unreal or super-real nature of public reality, whose presence simultaneously motivates and intimidates Gass's characters. Gass moves beyond their withdrawal because his are labors of love. The principal effect of Gass's art is to expand the world's offerings: "Paradoxically, every loving act of definition reverses the retreat of attention to the word and returns it to the world."[45] If the creation of art implies resistance of an incursion into the world, it is only to give the project an opportunity to flourish, not to achieve permanent exclusion. Investigating Gass's texts is a complex rescue mission meant to reclaim reality's subtlety and multifariousness, in the most positive sense of these words. Even though he is a consummate stylist, Gass still redeems his work from the narrowness of style for style's sake.

Admittedly, we have encountered many contemporary critics who, in their effusions over postrealist fiction, prescribe the use of language for no end other than displaying its inherent charms. Richard Gilman, for example, takes his cue from Alain Robbe-Grillet and Raymond Federman in arguing that the strained relationship between the world and art is an irrelevant concern, in that the isolated status of the text is really an acknowledgment of its self-validation; to surrender to a "confusion of realms" is to forget that art has "no reason for being other than to test and exemplify new forms of consciousness, which, moreover, have had to be invented precisely because actuality is incapable of generating them."[46] The occasion for this remark was his review of *Omensetter's Luck,* a novel which Gilman names "the most important work of fiction by an American in this literary generation,"[47] yet, in his opinion, its failing is in its vestigial attachments to literary convention: the trappings of traditional setting, character, and narrative line which he would reserve for the faint-hearted and the hopelessly reactionary among us. We may also be reminded of the often-quoted dictum of John Hawkes in which he indicts these familiar views of fiction as being "the true enemies of the novel."[48] Using the self-referentiality of language as a point of departure, this position equates the unreliability of fiction's "incorporative" powers with a justification of disengagement from the extra-textual reality of human affairs; additionally, literary hermeticism is exalted as allegiance to the imagination and as proof of liberation from the confining utilitarian strictures of realism. "From the perception . . . that literature has no objective truth, one moves to the conclusion that this is for the best, since objective truth is merely factual, boring, and middle-class."[49] And, so the presumption goes, in the sphere of uninterrupted consciousness can be found relief from inhibition.

But this is hardly an accurate appraisal of Gass's fictions. Autonomy is no great victory for Furber, Fender, or any of the other protagonists. On the contrary, their retreats are consistently portrayed as stifling, no matter what the attractions may be. Withdrawal is therefore unsuitable, psychologically as well as politically and socially. Gass himself recognizes that creative activity must ultimately lead to a repossession of the world and that the consolation of language must also attempt a reestablishment of connections if it is to prove viable on any grounds. It is far more useful to propose that if fiction is self-referential, it is not necessarily exclusively so; fiction can also depict the worldly conditions that have created the "givens" of contemporary American fiction which were the bases for vanguard writing.

Even a strong advocate of self-reflective fiction like Robert Alter warns against empty exercise and unrestrained self-indulgence on the part of certain authors who expect to be legitimized on the basis of having adopted the latest trend. While Alter goes so far as to prepare a comprehensive alternative canon for the novel, in which fictional form is "a consciously articulated entity rather than a transparent container of 'real' contents"[50]—he highlights the contributions of Cervantes, Fielding, Sterne, Diderot, Joyce, Woolf, Nabokov, and a host of postmodern adherents—he does not presume to excuse that tradition for an ignorance of history, time, society, and the life that surrounds its creation. Without this broader perspective, even the most ingeniously contrived novel will not avoid "a certain aridness; for the partial magic of the novelist's art, however self-conscious, is considerably more than a set of card tricks."[51] We know how stale superficial dazzlement can become when it is heralded as the primary goal of fiction. One memorable dissenting voice comes from John Barth's "Life-Story": "Another story about a writer writing a story! Another regressus in infinitum! Who doesn't prefer art that at least overtly imitates something other than its own processes? That doesn't continually proclaim "Don't forget I'm an artifice!"? That takes for granted its mimetic nature instead of asserting it in order (not so slyly after all) to deny it, or vice versa?"[52] The vitality of the most successful innovative fiction derives from the constant interplay and struggle between the imagined entity and those realities which challenge it.

Although Gass's narrators are loathe to tolerate such a substantial threat to their fictions, their author is not. Gass relinquishes neither the enchanting "physicality of words"[53] nor an understanding of the external reality which is art's ultimate context, and without which the most brilliant wordplay is rendered trivial. The intrigues and complexities of language merit our attention because they are features of broader socio-historical concerns. By presenting absurdity, elusiveness of meaning, and subjectivity of experience as both fictional symptoms and fictional subjects, Gass is answering the demands of those who refuse to compromise the "responsibilities" of art while at the same time making some of the most impressive contributions to art's current passion for probing its own structure.

In reassessing Gass's metaphor of the pointing statue, we wonder outward as well as travel back along the arm; moral, social, and aesthetic issues do not obscure but in fact reinforce one another. Clearly, an educated, sympathetic readership is required to undertake and understand these many issues, but it has always been the burden of great art to cultivate its own audience. According to William Gass, art refines consciousness so that it can measure up to the task of dealing with art. A more constrained vision of what art is and accomplishes underestimates its appeal: "If one insists on seeing all novels as congeries of semiotic systems intricately functioning in a pure state of self-referentiality, one loses the fine edge of responsiveness to the urgent human predicaments that novels seek to articulate. The greatness of genre, both in its realist and in its self-conscious modes, has been to present to us—through the most inventive variety of artifice, whether disguised or manifest—lives that might seem like our lives, minds like our minds, desires like our desires."[54]

The postrealists admonish us not to forget the integrity of the work of art as an object to be reckoned with apart from glib moral imperatives, but we should not diminish the profundity of the reading experience either. The intricate circuitry that develops between artwork and world is completed by the introduction of consciousness, which is in turn charged with increased sophistication. With regard to this model, albeit indirectly, Gass suggests his faith in the amenability of the world to examples of beauty and coherence, thereby granting the artist, whose artifice may instruct the world, a centrality that is foreign to Gass's narrators. While retaining the possibility that the creative consciousness can influence more than the shape of the isolated artwork, Gass asks that we become, in a far more positive, participatory way, artists of the beautiful. The key to "creative involvement with circumstance" is language, our means and proof of giving shape to the sensibilities of the self.[55] In the closing words of *Willie Masters' Lonesome Wife,* "Our tone should suit our time: uncommon quiet dashed with common thunder. It should be as young and quick and sweet and dangerous as we are. Experimental and expansive . . . it will give new glasses to new eyes, and put those plots and patterns down we find our modern lot in."[56]

2

Omensetter's Luck: The Fall into Language

WILLIAM GASS WARNS READERS of *Omensetter's Luck* not to be misguided by the title of his novel. His hero is not Bracket Omensetter, the "wide and happy man"[1] whose arrival in Gilean so profoundly indicts the drab, pedestrian lives of its townspeople; instead, "Furber is what the book turned out eventually to be all about," for it is he who survives through the medium of rhetoric. Reverend Jethro Furber dominates the novel because he most consistently carries forward Gass's principal theoretical considerations regarding the nature and function of literary art. "Omensetter is certainly not the major figure because he is basically a person without language. He is a wall everybody bounces a ball off. Now anybody who emerges in my work with any strength at all is somebody who has a language, and that's why he's there."[2] The "unnaturally natural"[3] Omensetter has no superficial layer; because he is "bracketed" by an inviolable innocence, he is that rare individual who feels free from the need to screen himself from reality with a saving artifice. Hence, his role in the novel is chiefly that of a device, a catalyst for action and psychological disruptions.

The main characters of the novel—Israbestis Tott, Henry Pimber, and Jethro Furber—are responsible for the generation of the novel's language. Each of their perceptions dominates a section of the novel, with the largest by far belonging to Furber, the most polished and professional monologist among them. All three must contend with the arrival of a man whose guiltless embrace of experience, whose uninhibited manner, and whose ability to exist in the world without abstracting it, simultaneously provoke their envy and their consternation, because in one way or another, Omensetter discloses their hemmed-in lifestyles as being paltry and unnourishing.

Faced with a living refutation of the need to stave off direct immersion in the natural world and to excuse their dispossession as the irrevocable human condition, each of the townspeople must either accept the inadequacy of his own resources in comparison to Omensetter's cryptic "luck" and relinquish the now-invalidated fiction he's been inhabiting, or spurn Omensetter as an enemy and bolster the fiction against the threat which the stranger represents. Unfortunately, the first alternative is not truly available in a post-Edenic world, in which everything from our suspicion of other people to our inevitable distance from our experiences is intensified by language itself; the fate of Henry Pimber confirms the tragic consequences of choosing to model oneself after the inimitable Omensetter. Therefore, the only resort is to disqualify Omensetter's effects on consciousness. In order to safeguard his intellectual refuge, Reverend Jethro Furber treats Omensetter as though he were a rabid animal and leads the popular reaction of Gilean against a man who must be deemed a devil if the continuance of the status quo is to be justified.

Through Furber's subversion, Omensetter's ease is redefined as sloth, his good fortune as demonism, and his benign indifference toward Pimber, who is found frozen and hanging from a tree limb, as murderous premeditation. Blissfully unaware of Furber's subterfuge, as he had been of Pimber's worship, Omensetter is quite vulnerable to the damage that words can do. Ironically, it is the man who is most isolated from the world, both physically behind his decaying garden walls and psychologically behind "his beautiful barriers of words," (p. 231) who brands Omensetter an outcast. In short, Omensetter must be condemned for blasphemy if Furber is to sustain his diametrically opposed circumstances. After a prolonged bout of convoluted reasoning, Furber sells himself on this conviction:

> *And what shall we conclude from all of this then?*
> *We must conclude he is the worst.*
> *He is the worst.*
> *Therefore.* (p. 156)

When Furber manages to expand his notion into a community-wide opinion, Omensetter falls prey to the relentless clutch of rhetoric and suffers a true separation from grace. He is reduced to the ordinary status of those who must rely on words to get by.

Israbestis Tott, the decrepit survivor of the novel's action, unpacks himself with words. "The Triumph of Israbestis Tott" is an ironic testimony to sheer endurance: he has managed, as promised, "to see the summer under" (p. 1). But his thoughts are sporadic and veer off indistinctly; he seems dazed and dislocated, an exile among strangers. Larry McCaffery correctly suggests that through the employment of Tott, Gass achieves the same rich ambiguity that Faulkner does by introducing *The Sound and the Fury* through Benjy's dream-like sense impressions, whose associations serve as poetic intimations that grow clearer only when we discover their attachments later in the novel.[4] Similarly, Tott inadvertently teaches us to doubt the substance of his own history, as Gass again emulates Faulkner by asserting that the rendition of the past is more of an artistic enterprise than a journalistic one. Every history is a justification and a pretense of certitude; however, history is less likely to actuate literal truth than the results of associations made by a subjective—and in Tott's case, an increasingly unstable—mind. Senility makes overt the human urge to schematize the past, so that through Tott we are introduced not only to significant characters and events, but also to the falsification that will always accompany their remembrance. Because they are filtered through an interpreting consciousness (a singularly, although not exclusively, questionable one in Tott's case), accumulated data arrive as material already formulated, inescapably pre-fictionalized.

Tott confounds our expectations when he views this paradox as an advantage. He emphasizes creativity over accuracy, or even consistency, in his storytelling; "real" history, as such, is useful solely because it contains materials to be exploited, although Tott glumly realizes that he has been losing his gift over time. At one point, for example, he disdains a nearby competitor: "Dull old fool, Israbestis thought, he's got no flair. I know these stories. Most of them are mine, my mouth gave each of them its shape, but I've no teeth to chew my long sweet youth again" (p. 6). The old stories lose their flavor when handled amateurishly.

In the manner of the auctioneer who is selling off the furnishings of the Pimber house, Tott takes inventory of the

names, incidents, and feelings that constitute his own and
Gilean's past. It would help us to consider a second literary
debt here, to Beckett's *Malone Dies,* to help us appreciate the
sole satisfaction left to an aged, forgotten man: namely, the
comfort of cataloguing one's possessions—his physical be-
longings and his memories. Obviously, the appeal of storytelling is that it gives the teller a sense of control while at the
same time earning him the dignity of being listened to. At
this point, however, Tott, who will later be described as "together beggar, hurdy-gurdy, cup, chain, monkey" (p. 67), is
a comical relic, and he can capture but briefly one boy's attention with the aid of the tale of Kick Shelton's cat. When
the boy has to leave—only the irrelevant have the luxury of
being able to permanently avoid worldly responsibilities—
Tott regrets the interruption of his "seduction" and calls it their
mutual loss: "Arrange . . . So I'll arrange . . . Well, he seemed
a nice boy, one of those our nowadays have lost. Too young
for the story of May Cobb. And how would he learn his history now? Imagine growing up in a world where only generals
and geniuses, empires and companies, had histories, not
your own town or grandfather, house or Samantha—none of
the things you'd loved" (pp. 26–27). The grubby world of
facts is no match for the fabulous, and it may be another aspect of Tott's triumph that he has been privileged to escape
for a time into the latter. Tott makes a perpetual effort to
bring confusion and fear under the control of "a composed
plausibility."[5] In his unique way, Tott participates in art's
raid upon disorder; perhaps to his misfortune, of course, is the
fact that the very imagination which recoils from disruptions
in the stories of the past contributes to the chaos by continuing
to invent, edit, and reconsider. Almost involuntarily, the storyteller undermines stability even as he is striving to attain it.

On returning to the dismantling of our faith in narrative reliability, we should note that the fanciful attributes of words, which Tott relishes, militate against their capacity for documentation. Indeed, our upcoming encounter with Brackett Omensetter, who will be repeatedly described in terms of nature's abundant mysteries, is prejudiced because of Tott's admission that the weird commiseration between Kick's magnificently hungry cat and his surroundings is "nothing you could put in words" (p. 20). Like the cat, Omensetter is part of a mythic reality which is immune to language; all namegiving fails to describe such beings who operate instinctively, outside of language, and the attempt to assign titles to them merely emphasizes the futility of doing so. "Cats know how to live," Tott muses. "Cats beat us at it bad. Now Brackett Omensetter, though—" (p. 23).

The past teases Tott to the limits of comprehension, ever-receding beyond his undependable intellectual grasp. More to his liking is "life in the wall," a painstakingly elaborate fiction he plays out in his delicious solitude. This is Tott at his most lyrical, where his congeries are most nearly purged of the historical content that directs his public storytelling. The wall offers itself to him like an unsoiled canvas, and every ridge and crack spurs enchantment:

You could imagine maps in the wall paper. The roses had faded into vague shells of pink. Only a few silver lines along the vanished stems and in the veins of leaves, indistinct patches of the palest green, remained—the faint suggestion of mysterious geography. A grease spot was a marsh, a mountain or a treasure. Israbestis went boating down a crack on cool days, under the tree boughs, bending his head. He fished in a chip of plaster. The perch rose to the bait and were golden in the sunwater. Specks stood for cities; pencil marks were bridges; stains and shutter patterns laid out fields of wheat and oats and corn. In the shadow of a corner the crack issued into a great sea. There was a tear in the paper that looked exactly like a railway and another that signified a range of hills. Some tiny drops of ink formed a chain of lakes. A darker decorative strip of Grecian pediments and interlacing ivy at the ceiling's edge kept the tribes of Gog and Magog from invasion. Once he had passed through it to the ceiling but it made him dizzy and afraid (pp. 10–11).

Tott allows his imagination to range far beyond the small-town boundaries of "the old slow world" (p. 13) and transcends his own physical debilities. But he still cannot entirely repudiate external reality, even in private fantasy; the fact that he views his limited access to "real" details as a draw-back to his fictional journeys betrays his continuing reliance upon the outside world for legitimation, just as he judges the value of his stories according to the responsiveness of his audience.

Hence, Tott is compromised on two fronts. Those stories derived from Gilean's past are a hodgepodge of narrative bits which only become decipherable later in the novel; in fact, several of them are never mentioned again in *Omensetter's Luck* (such as the Hen Wood's fire) even though Tott conjures them in the same breath as information whose significance is revealed in time. The point is that Tott's desire to preserve the past, if only for its narrative possibilities, is frustrated by the undifferentiated clutter that memory has become for him: "Yes. There was a story. No. That wasn't Lutie Root. She had a harder eye, as hard an eye as her old man had, like translucent rock. She went in the winter. He'd forgot. Hard eye and all, paler and paler till it went out. Who were all these people?" (p. 3) Somehow he forgot there were Italians. In those days there weren't many. Sometimes they came to repair the railroad. Or were they Mexicans? Sicilians? Did it make a difference?" (pp. 4–5) Gass's artist is, above all, a craftsman in complete control of his materials; the confusion that infests Tott's reclamation work on his old stories disqualifies him as an artist who can employ the world meaningfully. This is his first failure. His second is his inability to withdraw into an artifice that is not contingent upon the "facts," or that does not depend upon objective confirmation for its adequacy. Whatever transcendent adventures in the wall offer dissolves when he discovers that, here again, his memory is found wanting. More than once the boy who revels in the wonders of Kick's cat points out that the story could have been improved if Tott had surrendered completely to flights of imagination:

> I bet he knew everything about trains and stations.
> He knew everything about trains and stations.
> I bet he knew when trains got to Chicago, Illinois.
> He knew when trains did anything.
> I bet he was fierce as anything, like a turkey.
> Turkeys aren't very fierce.
> I hate turkeys. They gobble at you.
> Well Kick's cat was fiercer than that.
> I bet. I bet he could fly.
> Of course he couldn't.
> He could.
> No.
> At night. At night he could.
> Say, who knows about this cat, boy, you or me? (p. 24)

Were Tott to practice what he preaches—the primacy of "flair" over realistic precision as a criterion for evaluating fiction—he might very well be satisfied with his creations. (By contrast, William Gass sets his novel in late nineteenth-century Ohio, about which he was purposefully unfamiliar during the composition of *Omensetter's Luck,* so as to be unencumbered by preexistent realistic information.) However, as evidenced by the story of Kick's cat, he cannot let go completely of traditional demands on art, and that is exactly where the flaws in the artifice are flagrant: "He was conscious, always, of the inadequacy of his details, the vagueness of his pictures, the falsehood in all his implicit etceteras, because he knew nothing, had studied nothing, had traveled nowhere. Consequently, he was never fully in the bedclothes, clawing at the skin of his legs and biting his arms. He was only partly bowed by rain or sand, or sleet, crouched before the attack of lions or wild tribesmen, swimming for his life. The pain struck without obstruction then, and he closed like a spider on it" (p. 12).

The spider metaphor which concludes this passage is recurrent in Tott's section; it is the artist who survives by confining its victims, as Tott lures his listeners, within its intricate workmanship. But Tott is a spider tangled in his fictions. The "triumph" ends with Tott crushing a "nasty" spider with his thumb, symbolically uniting his limited and limiting brand of art with death. However, his final victory is hollow. Death will close upon Tott soon enough, and because his art has confused, rather than preserved, the years, it, too, is in jeopardy; the crazy mutterings of a deluded ancient will expire along with him. He is left at an impasse of his own making: "Tott—you've shut your house. In effect, you've shut your house. You can't forget, and you don't dare remember" (p. 28). Tott the historian cannot wholly communicate; Tott the fabricator cannot wholly create. Prefiguring Furber, he fails to serve the world either as a custodian of local history or as a celebrant of autonomy. Because the outpouring of language is as likely to remind the novel's narrators of their having lost the density of life as it is to provide sufficient compensation for that loss, we could accuse all of the novel's narrators of demolishing their hideaways with the very words they use to establish them. To comfort oneself with the validity of a verbal substitute as frequently as Tott and Furber do belies the contentment it presumably offers.

Having aroused our suspicions about the motives underlying narration, Gass turns his focus to the main story. During the course of the novel, many of the salient conflicts which characterize American literature arise—Good versus Evil, Nature versus Civilization, Innocence versus Experience— and therefore promote a sense of familiarity. These conflicts, however, must be reevaluated in view of the fact that they suggest simplistic dichotomies which the subjective consciousness foists upon the mystery of Brackett Omensetter. Gass himself conditions us to expect the artist to prefer the decorous to the desultory and the arranged to the accurate. His artist comes closest to being a scientist, not in the results he obtains but in his impulse to quantify: "The movements everywhere around us—in us—seem, well . . . too numerous, too vague, too fragile and transitory to number, and that's terribly unsettling, for we always feel threatened when confronted with something we can't count. Why should we be surprised, then, to find out that creating and defending a connection between what William James called the buzzing, blooming confusion of normal consciousness—of daily life with its unstimulating bumps, its teaseless, enervating grinds—and the clear and orderly silences of mathematics, a connection which will give us meaning, security, and management, in one lump sum, is what our science—is what our art, law, love and magic—is principally about"?[6]

And no method of narration systematizes data better than the tall tale. It is the formula story, the capsular cliché, that promises immediate gratification in the form of recognizable categories of meaning. Brackett Omensetter is introduced as a myth, with the requisite prefatory awe: "Brackett Omensetter was a wide and happy man. He could whistle like the cardinal whistles in the deep snow, or whirr like the shy 'white rising from its cover, or be the lark a-chuckle at the sky. He knew the earth. He put his hands in water. He smelled the clean fir smell. He listened to the bees. And he laughed his deep, loud, wide and happy laugh whenever he could—which was often, long, and joyfully" (p. 31). From the beginning, any conception of Omensetter the man is obstructed by the predilections of Henry Pimber, his would-be disciple. (Nor can we anticipate any reliable clarification from Rev. Furber, since he will interpose an altogether different bias of his own.) The "love and sorrow" which Omensetter brings to Pimber would be remarkable solely for the reason that such a man as Pimber could be moved to deep feeling at all. At first, Pimber sees Omensetter as the quintessential fool just begging to be taken advantage of, and Pimber complies by renting the unwitting man and his pregnant wife a house that floods when it rains. And yet, it is the landlord who is overwhelmed by their initial meeting. From the shy, disheveled stranger emanates a nameless power that stuns Pimber into amazement: "Sweetly merciful God, Henry wondered, sweetly merciful God, what has struck me?" (p. 37)

Omensetter's obliviousness to the burdens of daily life occasions ridicule and disbelief until it becomes apparent that he has a talent for survival that excuses carelessness. Inexplicably, his house remains unflooded despite Pimber's conviction that it rained more than it had in years; a deep splinter in Omensetter's thumb causes only mild, detached notice; and an accidental blow from Mat Watson's hammer earns only a wordless smile. Like a fairy-tale magician, Omensetter reads the signs that foretell the sex of his child, and then accepts their fruition matter-of-factly, as though he had predicted nightfall. Pimber's astonishment turns to indignation at one so steadfastly primitive: "He stored his pay in a sock which hung from his bench, went about oblivious of either time or weather, habitually permitted things which he'd collected like a schoolboy to slip through holes in his trousers. He kept worms under saucers, stones in cans, poked the dirt all the time with twigs, and fed squirrels navy beans and sometimes noodles from his hands. Broken tools bemused him; he often ate lunch with his eyes shut; and, needless to say, he laughed a lot. He let his hair grow; he only intermittently shaved; who knew if he washed; and when he went to pee, he simply let his pants drop" (p. 40). "That man," as Furber dismisses him, "lives like a cat asleep in a chair" (p. 44), reminding us of Tott's comparison of Omensetter to Kick's cat. In short, he is seen to be less than normal at this stage: his natural harmony is equated with stupefaction, and his silence is defined as a vacuum.

Nevertheless, Pimber's obsession with Omensetter belies his outward scorn. Even though he insists that Omensetter is "inhuman as a tree" (p. 67), Pimber cannot conceal from himself that he envies that condition; he sees in Omensetter an example of escape from a life cramped with abstraction and consumed with self-consciousness—in Hamlet's phrase, enclosed in a pale cast of thought. Humanity is identified by the compulsion to assess itself; consciousness verifies our post-lapsarian state of removal from an insensate natural environment. Our distinction from mindless matter causes ambivalence, for as George Steiner postulates, the breaking free from the legacy of nature

is both miracle and outrage, sacrament and blasphemy. It is sharp severance from the world of the animal, man's begetter and sometime neighbor, the animal who, if we rightly grasp the myths of centaur, satyr, and sphinx, has been inwoven with the very substance of man, and whose instinctive immediacies and shapes of physical being have receded only partially from our own form. This harsh weaning, of which antique mythology is so uneasily conscious, has left its scars. Our own new mythologies take up the theme: in Freud's grim imitation of man's backward longing of his covert wish for re-immersion in an earlier, inarticulate state of organic existence; in Claude Levi-Strauss's speculations on man's self-banishment by his Promethian theft of fire (the choice of cooked over raw food), and by his mastery of speech, from the natural rhythms and anonymities of the animal world.[7]

Perception must function as consolation for our distance from nature, from God, and from our own senses, and one accommodates himself to that distance by accepting it as the inevitable result, in religious terms, of our expulsion from Eden. And yet, Brackett Omensetter, who lived instead of observed life, who had the secret of "joining himself to what he knew" (p. 69), strikes Pimber as a walking exception to the rule of distance. When Omensetter's homemade poultice cures Pimber's lockjaw, which had resisted the remedies of Doctor Orcutt and the prayers of Reverend Furber, the devotion of Henry Pimber is assured. Perhaps Omensetter's luck is a commodity which can be shared, his serenity "a dream you might enter" (p. 47).

Henry Pimber is the Everyman of the novel. His plight and his desire result from an awareness of the Fall which the seemingly unaffected Omensetter aggravates. Therefore, Pimber's first reflex is to discredit Omensetter. Eventually, however, Pimber's desire for self-abandonment gets the better of his suspicions: "Not Adam but inhuman. Was that why he loved him, Henry wondered. It wasn't for his life—a curse, God knew; it wasn't for the beet-root poultice. It lay somewhere in the chance of being new . . . of living lucky, and of losing Henry Pimber" (p. 67). Neighbors and friends pale before his eyes, thereby sickening him; if Omensetter is the mysterious cause, he determines, he may also be the cure.

Of course, the conventional wisdom is that the unification of the self and the sublime is engineered through religious faith, and in this sense, Pimber becomes a point of contention between the opposing claims upon the human soul symbolized by Omensetter and Furber. Furber recognizes the significance of "winning" Pimber, and he applies his verbal weaponry to the challenge, denigrating Omensetter as satanic because he ignores orthodoxy while simultaneously inviting people to cast aside their humanity (as proved by the "spell" he has obviously woven around Pimber). But during Pimber's illness, it is Omensetter's rather than Furber's influence which clearly dominates. Omensetter's manner is clearly the more inviting. Contrary to the mysterious stranger, who is always described in various states of physical ease; Furber is described as knotted, twisted, and locked in: while Omensetter calmly applies his poultice, "Furber hung like a drapery demonstrating him, his hollow—all could see it, billowing thinly, the wall gauze, and God's laws flickering" (p. 50). Even Pimber's wife, who accuses her transformed husband of being possessed in some unimaginable way, cannot sanction the meddling of so unsavory a character as Furber: "Or is it the Furber preaching at you, trying to fish your soul out like the last pickle?" (p. 53)

As it happens, what Furber cannot secure with numerous machinations of language, Omensetter captures without realizing. Unfortunately, the very state of unconcern which seduces Pimber, denies him access to the "miracle" of how to be. Quite simply, Omensetter is as oblivious to Pimber's worship as nature is to a poet's ode. Meanwhile, Pimber courts an acquaintance that Omensetter cannot appreciate, leaving

Pimber in a far more anxious state than he was prior to Omensetter's arrival in Gilean:

> It was since his sickness . . . Everything began with—since his sickness. Once to petrify and die had been his wish; simply to petrify had been his fear; but he had been a stone with eyes and seen as a stone sees: the world as the world is really, without the least prejudice of heart or artifice of mind, and he had come into such truth as only a stone can stand. He yearned to be hard and cold again and have no feeling, for since his sickness he'd been preyed upon by dreams, sleeping and waking, and by sudden rushes of unnaturally sharp, inhuman vision in which all things were dazzling, glorious, and terrifying. He saw then, he thought, as Omensetter saw, except for painful beauty. If there were just a way to frighten off the pain (p. 66).

Whereas Pimber's mundane existence was once merely a dull routine, now the need for salvation has been kindled and the spiritual wilderness he inhabits has grown conspicuous and agonizing. Not even words can help him any longer. The names of trees echo "in his lonely skull" and actually intensify his feeling of separation from them —once again, in contrast to Omensetter's preternatural capacity for joining himself to his surroundings.[8] Trying to talk to Omensetter one last time, Pimber is deafened and terrified by the noise of the wind, so that even shouting does not establish contact. Only after it is too late does he discover that he cannot apprentice himself to a man whose luck—he did not have the words to analyze Omensetter's gift precisely—was based upon his being immune to trials of conscious perception. Omensetter "knows" no secret; Pimber is excluded by definition.

Pimber vaguely comprehended his fate earlier, when the futility of hoping to absorb Omensetter's unconscious ease made him feel foolish. "Necessity flew birds as easily as the wind drove these leaves, and they never felt the curvature which drew the arc of their pursuit. Nor would a fox cry beauty before he chewed" (p. 69). Here he is recalling the incident which had been nagging him since it occurred: having snatched a hen in its jaws, a fox tumbled down an open well. To Pimber's surprise, Omensetter and his children laugh at the trapped creature and leave it to die, apparently content to let nature run its course without interference. Pimber, however, identifies himself with the fallen animal, reading it as an allegorical message meant for him. Thus, he transfers his own fear of neglect and falls prey to self-mocking doubt:

> Ding dong bell.
> Pimber's down our well.
> . . . .
> Who pushed him in?
> Little Henry Pim.
> . . . .
> Who'll pull him out?
> Nobody's about.
> . . . .
> What a naughty thing was that,
> To catch our little Pimber at,
> Who never did him any harm,
> But . . . (pp. 45–46).

Pimber returns to shoot the fox and board up the well. Larry McCaffery argues convincingly that the action is at once symbolic of his forthcoming suicide, when Omensetter once again ignores a fallen victim, and of a desire to revenge himself upon Omensetter for his indifference.[9] (To carry this further, we can see him as the "Hennie" caught in Omensetter's pitiless clutches.) Interestingly, Pimber is originally somewhat detached from the fox, viewing it as something alien whose feelings can barely be guessed at. In doing so, and thereby distancing himself from the animal that "filled up the edges of its body like a lake" (p. 43), Pimber uses the same sort of metaphor that is often applied to Omensetter, who likewise lives completely and instinctively. In other words, Pimber confirms his essential difference from Omensetter. When he begins to confer consciousness—his consciousness—upon the fox, the distance between perceiver and perceived closes, but does not free him from his predicament: "He had never measured off his day in moments: another—another—another. But now, thrown down so deeply in himself, into the darkness of the well, surprised by pain and hunger, might he not revert to an earlier condition, regain capacities which formerly were useless to him, pass from animal to Henry, become human in his prison, X his days, count, wait, listen for another—another—another—another?" (p. 46)

The logic of these considerations demotes Pimber to the level of a lower life form to be sloughed off or evolved out of. Pimber's suicide represents his final revulsion toward the harshness of an unfiltered awareness of the human situation, according to which, awareness itself is a prison. Omensetter's influence coaxes Pimber into abandoning his defenses—whatever methods people employ to stave off an unprotected vision of the world—for a false hope: "Everybody but the preacher stole from him. Furber merely hated. But what I took was hope—a dream—fool's gold—quarrel—toothsome hen, Henry said" (pp. 72–73). He believes that he has been made the butt of a practical joke, and he tempers regret with black humor: he chooses to reverse the death of the fox, his spiritual double, by hanging dead from a tall tree limb instead of down a dark hole, complimenting himself on the pun of "leave-taking." Therefore, in the end, Pimber abstracts impending death by poeticizing it as relentlessly as he did Omensetter. The resort to language verifies the post-lapsarian status of mankind once again.

Through a studied, deliberate change of perspective, Jethro Furber determines that the artificial life circumscribed by language is adequate, if not abundant, recompense for the sacrifice of direct contact with the world. Because he is able to consolidate an image of consciousness as a fortress instead of a trap, Furber survives Omensetter's implicit challenge where Pimber could not. As mentioned earlier, Furber defuses the threat to his fiction by robbing Omensetter of any relevance for humanity. To grant Omensetter admiration, much less envy or eminence, would be blasphemous, at least according to Furber. Since Omensetter has already demonstrated the ability to topple people's doctrines, Furber quickly outfits his God against him; whereas Pimber saw Omensetter's distance from common man as man as transcendence, Furber calls it exile, and what Pimber perceived as grace, the Reverend reviles publically as sin.

Furber presides over a society he can shape to his rhetoric. On the other hand, Omensetter's effect on his neighbors is sensational without being influential; he cannot transform them by quietly radiating natural harmony into the atmosphere. Therefore, Furber's insinuations that Pimber was actually murdered by this bizarre intruder—Omensetter—are decisive, and they have the added attraction of restoring the confidence which the people of Gilean had lost at the hands of Omensetter. (To personify evil and then cast evil out both purifies and validates the environment.) Under Furber's supervision, the magical properties that had been attributed to Omensetter are replaced by satanic ones, and Omensetter himself is but a human mirror, helpless to do other than reflect the desires and apprehensions of whoever perceives him.

Still, Omensetter's staggering composure does not capitulate to public opinion; his obliviousness to gossip or conjecture, as we have seen, is one of his salient personality traits. It is when his luck surfaces as a conscious phenomenon in his own mind—when he begins to know his grace instead of simply living it—that he loses its privileges. "He had an ease impossible to imitate," Pimber reflected, "for the moment you were aware, the instant you tried." (p. 46). Pimber noticed his hero's contamination by consciousness shortly before the suicide. His disappointment in Omensetter's susceptibility to mediocrity made Pimber pity him as he did himself and all of mankind for the same affliction (p. 73). To mollify Lucy when their infant son contracts diptheria, Omensetter tells her to trust in his luck, but he proves its absence with this verbal acknowledgment of it—a contradiction of what had once been innate and unspoiled by words. "And now he knows," thinks Furber. "There's no further injury that we can do them—his wife or the girls. They will live on like we live, most likely" (p. 301).

From this rare admission of sympathy from the rigorously self-consumed Furber, we can ascertain that the fervor with which he assails the stranger, although it is precipitated by the need to defend the integrity of his calling, is merely a consolation for his not enjoying the blessings of instinctive harmony. Marcel Raymond, in *From Baudelaire to Surrealism,* offers a relevant analysis of the search for compensation among the Symbolist poets, who may be seen as precursors to Furber in their attempts to reify through language a surrogate form of the perfect happiness of Eden. Its absence leaves man "with an even more acute awareness of his limitations and of the precariousness of his life. He will not rest until he has again forced the gates of Paradise, or if this is impossible, until he has profited from these revelations . . . . The soul engages in a kind of game, but aspires to an activity that is more elevated than any game—aspires to recreate its lost happiness by means of the *word*".[10] Furber cannot rid himself entirely of the sense of surrogacy that infects his love of words. He does not completely overcome the "feverish love" of his congregation for Omensetter, and he realizes that he does envy the man he is committed to destroy: "Well, why not? Natural. Who hadn't envy of the animals? He had, certainly, his share. They were the trunk of his life—these envious feelings" (p. 136).

Although he openly decries Omensetter as dangerously inhuman, Furber himself came to Gilean under vaguely scandalous circumstances, apparently having committed some trespass in his previous position. We glean from Furber's ruminations that his has been a lifelong retreat from the strenuous demands of the world. The church was a logical career, not because of any dedication to piety, but because it was a socially acceptable means of withdrawal. Indeed, Furber's sexual preoccupations, though they are limited to the intellect, crowd out the spiritual speculations we would expect from a clergyman. We learn of several episodes from his adolescence which emphasize a denial of healthy outlets for emotional expression. While he was a frail child, Furber was afraid of the world's "noise"; ironically, his parents' dedication to protecting him from demanding encounters ensured that he would not develop the capacity for operating in the world. The most obvious indication of this is his transference of sexual desire: apart from isolated liberties allowed by a neighborhood girl and his Aunt Janet, young Furber turns to explicit passages in the Bible for sexual fulfillment. As he reaches maturity, his fantasies grow more complex and aloof, until, clearly, language supplants feeling altogether. In short, Furber manages a reverse transubstantiation of the flesh into the Word. The result is a systematic perversion of human nature, as is powerfully displayed during Furber's trip to Gilean when he accosts the girl sitting beside him by laying his shadow upon her. From then on, onanism defines his lifestyle as well as his sexual character: "Surfaces. Scatters. He'd kept everything at word's length, and it was words he saw when he saw her—tight, and white, and shining; it was words he felt when his anger burned him, when he shook and wailed and struck about wildly. Out of the world he could safely take just the ravelings: the color of the bruise on his toe, for instance, or the isolated croak of a frog which surprises the afternoon, or the vision of an intense green slope where a ball coasts under a wicket. Though mankind was his hobby—so he'd often said—he knew nothing of men" (p. 230).

Time and again, Furber insists that language is his only arena of achievement, and consequently, that it is superior to the life for which it substitutes. He deems his word barriers beautiful (p. 231), and is positively enraptured by the sexual surrogacy of speech: "The ladies egged him on; in Eve's name, they dared him; so he made love with discreet verbs and light nouns, delicate conjunctions. They begged; they defied him to define . . . define everything. They could not be scandalized—impossible, they said. Indecent prepositions such as in, on, up, merely made them smile, and the roundest exclamation broke upon them like a bubble's kiss, a butterfly's. Smooth and creamy adjectives enabled them to lick their lips upon the crudest story" (pp. 202–3). Through preaching, Furber maintains a strictly qualified contact with other people; caressing them with words, he earns a measured access and vents his lust with relative impunity. Nevertheless, when he sees Lucy Omensetter unabashedly sunning herself by the water, imagination plagues instead of soothes him. Human nature is not always controllable, and the inflamed Furber condemns his voyeurism as personal weakness. He occasionally wishes he could slap backs, talk fishing, play the banjo. Is there not something dishonest, he wonders, about a life lived discreetly under God when it isolates one from the community? The preacher keeps up the required appurtenances of "secular" interest—he does not neglect his congregation in ways that would arouse suspicion and jeopardize his position—but it is pretense only. He is in love with the form of his sermons, not with the audience he addresses. As Gass explains, since "there is no out-of-doors in the world where language is the land,"[11] Furber readily and consistently excuses his betrayal of the outside world. (Many of Gass's characters in later fictions will inherit from Furber the anxiety to justify their linguistic privacies by championing the value of the expression for its own sake, which evokes, in a phrase from "Carrots, Noses, Snow, Rose, Roses," its "true muteness.")[12]

Furber's mismanagement of language, for all its pleasures, strips words of their communicability by switching their function from contacting the exterior world to buttressing and decorating the interior substitute. But the sacrifice goes well beyond simply foregoing the trivialities of ordinary existence; it has a corrosive effect on one's being:

The limits of our communicable world are the limits of our lives. In our communication with one another we mediate, on the one hand, the form and the substance of our consciousness, on the other, the form and significance of all of our social arrangements and social institutions. We create ourselves and recreate the social/cultural milieu in which we will have our lives, in communication. Just as our histories are a matter of what we have said of them, our futures are a matter of what we may say of them.

Every human culture, every human society, every human encounter, every human being, must be *realized* in communication.
What we refer to when we refer to "human nature" is nowhere to
be found in nature. It is what people have made of themselves, in
various cultures, at different times and in different ways, in and
through communication.[13]

To break off negotiations with the world by stifling one's
approach to it, and one's input from it, through language, is
to shrink the self even as one thinks he is fortifying it.
Furber's ingenious interpretation of his religion excuses his
idiosyncracies, but it corrupts human nature: "It was sad,
but churches rarely lived so largely. They were seldom permitted such extravagance of feeling. In fact, they were—at
least his was—a sour denial of the human spirit. He caught
himself quickly. He'd meant, of course, that they were a so-
ber condemnation of the evil in human nature . . . something different. However he was a notorious liar" (pp. 171–
72). An objective view of Furber's walled-in garden reveals it
to be a false version of paradise. The sanctuary is overgrown
with decaying vines and the lock is rusted. Although he reasons that the value of a wall is based on its ability to "blind
and deafen," no inspiration can penetrate these thickets
either. The suffocative garden is the physical equivalent of his
rhetoric-infested consciousness. A "clean, vibrant world of
aesthetics,"[14] where Furber can exercise his imagination un-
observed, the garden is also a prisonhouse whose walls delim-
it his gratifications. Furthermore, the garden is also haunted
by the ghost of Rev. Pike, Furber's predecessor, for whom the
current preacher's confessions are reserved. "Joy to be a
stone," Furber declares when his feelings threaten to get the
best of him in front of witnesses; he aspires to that same condition of emotionless opacity, the comfort of not being suf-

fused with sense. He will secretly compliment Henry Pimber for attaining freedom through suicide, while for the time being, he confers with the dead.

Enter Brackett Omensetter, who infuses stones with life. Skipping stones across the water, or sending horseshoes into the air, Omensetter entices Furber with the posssibility of transcendence of human mortality: "He sent them aloft and the heart rose with them, wondering if they'd ever come back they seemed so light" (p. 144). Like Pimber, Furber is "teased" by "a dream you could enter"—life without regret and numbing self-awareness, and open to genuine sensuality; however, Furber arrests himself where Pimber could not. Furber sees how Omensetter only tricks the stones into temporary weightlessness—"There's no help for it, they have to come down to a stone's end" (p. 145)—so that by generating false hopes, Omensetter actually intensifies our knowledge of the fact that, trapped in our own heaviness, we must surely sink into our graves. The Devil himself perpetrates no viler deception.

This is the logic that enables Furber to charge his psychological distrust of Omensetter with theological resolve. "We must conclude he is the worst" is but an indication of Furber's defense mechanism in action. Omensetter is the personification of the preacher's real wish for himself. Furber had been able to create the precarious rationalization that the instinctive life is unsuitable for mankind, and he consoled himself with the trappings of a "higher calling" until Omensetter arrived on the scene to force him to see the poverty of his fiction. By destroying Omensetter, Furber hopes to smash a hateful mirror.

Furber plans to poison public opinion against a man whose influence, because it is not completely comprehensible, is not trusted. Seen from a slightly different perspective, Furber is an artist who abuses the artist's power to modify the consciousness of his audience. He reduces the wonder of Omensetter to a symbol to be manipulated inside a fiction; he then convinces the townspeople to invest in the same fictional premises he does. Gass has noted that it is erroneous and perilous "to treat people in terms of symbol systems only," as though aesthetic and ethical stances could be interchanged without consequence.[15] Whereas we applaud the artist's talent for composing his creation in a manner which achieves the most telling effects, we must not confuse the license the artist has within a fictional context with his freedom to be capricious in the world. "Betrayed by form," artist and audience alike may be tempted into ethical disaster. "Just as there are many things we can attribute to persons that we cannot logically attribute to characters, characters too have attributes that we cannot, dare not, grant to persons. We cannot and should not try to author persons or to destroy them whimsically: to pick them up, put them down, and contemplate their condition with disinterested curiosity. This category mistake (to use the philosophical name for it) is the chief concern of much of Gass's fiction; it is the distinction that his villains override and what brings his victims to their grief."[16] Omensetter's presence spills through the restrictive concept that Furber has constructed to contain him; nevertheless, by replacing the man with the model in the Gileanite mind, Furber trumps reality. Put another way, he exteriorizes his dependency on his fiction and raises it to a normative level.

Paranoia directed outward takes the form of propaganda. Furber encourages a symbolic view of Omensetter as a material target for universal fears. Significant is Northrop Frye's contention that modern alienation renders us very susceptible to this sort of manipulation, and our anxiety over having lost a sense of control over our own destinies encourages us to believe in a "tyrant-enemy," or Devil. It is only natural under these circumstances to want to project that evil outward; otherwise, the self is implicated and held culpable for evil and we resultantly suffer from a death-wish.[17] Certainly Furber displays this obsession when he ponders the "message" of Pimber's suspended corpse: "So it is with us. So it is with me. So. So. It is so like. Buried in this air, I rot. Moment by moment, I am not the same. And all I desire is to escape—get out" (p. 256). And in his essay on suicide, "The Doomed in Their Sinking," Gass indirectly refers to his language-loving protagonist: "If we are to call suicide every self-taken way out of the world, then even the Platonic pursuit of knowledge, involving as it does the separation of reason from passion and appetite, is suicidal . . . as are, of course, the search for ecstatic states, and longings for mystical unions."[18] How transparent is Furber's worship of stones in this light! Little wonder, then, to see Furber convince the people of Gilean to help him seize upon Omensetter as a means of deflecting his self-destructiveness. Imbedded in the preacher's sermons is an additional religious endorsement of anti-Omensetter sentiment. Furber appropriates the technique common to advertising, politics, and other forms of mass appeal, which is "to stun and demoralize the critical consciousness with statements too absurd or extreme to be dealt with seriously by it. In the mind that is too frightened or credulous or childish to want to deal with the world at all, they move in past the consciousness and set up their structures unopposed.

What they create in such a mind is not necessarily acceptance, but dependence on their versions of reality."[19]

Ironically, Omensetter contributes to the "plot" to drive himself out. He does this by confiding to Furber, his persecutor, that he has discovered Pimber's body in the forest. This is the novel's climactic episode, for at this instance both men become their most fully human. Omensetter descends into common human anxiety about the frailties of man's physical state, while Furber is moved to slacken his efforts to saddle Omensetter with responsibility for Pimber's death because he is touched by the majesty of the man's innocence. Suddenly the supplicating Omensetter affects Furber not as some conveniently abstracted symbol but directly, as a human being. Omensetter's desperate faith in him shocks Furber into uncharacteristic openness and recognition: "The fool. Come safely to me? The idiot. I'm safety? Where—where have you been? My god. My god. A friend. I've spent my life spreading lies about you. A friend, eh? a friend, a friend—" (p. 240). Not disdain, now, but yearning sets the tone of that "Where have you been?" Furber even addresses him by his correct name (Brackett instead of Backett, which had been his custom) because for once, he sees the man instead of the aberration he has concocted. Furber also sees that he has been wrong about love, having discriminated against it and spread lies about it all his life in the service of principles that do not hold up in face of Omensetter's remarkable grace.[20] The coherence of his sermons—the security of "the world seen from a mountain" (p. 214)—pales into insignificance.

The critical illness of Omensetter's son confirms for both men the bankruptcy of their respective separations from ordinary social intercourse. Omensetter had always enjoyed a natural isolation that neither scorn nor fear could penetrate—until now, when crisis visits his own household. He calls upon his luck to save him, counting upon his affiliation with nature, but as stated earlier, the fact that he has been educated into a verbal awareness of his luck steeps him in common human perception. Dazedly, with the baby suffering in its cradle, he makes animal shadows on the wall with the same hands that had once convinced Mat Watson that they could work magic with leather. Watching the diminished, helpless man, "Furber had the impression of something being poured steadily through a hole in the floor" (p. 254), again reminding us of the metaphor of the trapped fox.

With as much regret as consternation, Furber derides the befuddled Omensetter for the irrelevance of his personality to obligations that have closed in upon him: "Look: if a bird were to rub its beak on a limb, you'd hear it—sure—and if a piece of water were to move an unaccustomed way, you'd feel it—that's right—and if a fox were to steal a hen, you'd see— you'd see it —even in the middle of the night; but, heaven help you, if a friend a friend—god—were to slit your throat with his—his love—hoh, you'd bleed a week to notice it" (p. 241). Yes, Omensetter must be held accountable for Pimber's death, for his son's illness, even for Furber's dismay, because ignorance does not excuse his catalytic role in each case.

As for Furber, he has only speeches to offer, and they are hollow gestures—the vain "wig-wag" of a practiced "ringaling tongue" (p. 263). Since he had never truly used words to express religious conviction or to grant solace to others, but simply to fashion a "blindfold," he can only delineate the long record of his failure to live. Lovelessness has created a monster diseased by sound: "You're an old man already, Furber. You've been shaken half out of life by the effort of living in it. Ah, that would do to preach. Oh shut your shit" (pp. 271–72).

Omensetter mutely collects stones into a circle—he can barely understand his need to pray—and in doing so mimics Furber's reliance on sanctuary.[21] He is also trying to restore his old powers over nature, as he hoped to do previously by examining his hands, which had once animated stones. But it is an empty exercise. When Furber witnesses Omensetter's ritual, he is so exasperated that he kicks apart the structure. Perhaps he has realized the injury one can do to himself by cringing behind barriers, since life behind his own walls of words has turned him into a "pale, pinch-faced little man . . . the nail-eyed reverend" (p. 76), utterly removed from "the conscience of his people" and deteriorated to the point that he is fit only for the company of ghosts. We may choose to remember Robert Frost's "Mending Wall" and its silent admonishment to the gruff neighbor: "Before I built a wall I'd ask to know/What I was walling in or walling out."[22] The profound consequences of worldly events deny the luxury of irresponsibility in the end. Doc Orcutt, who is wholly *of* the world instead of provisionally like Furber or tentatively like Omensetter, proves to be the child's last and best chance for survival. To be returned to the world, one requires relevant attention. Diptheria is "no theological disease" (p. 264), nor is it some fatal witchery to be controverted by white magic.

Furber rails at Omensetter for his inactivity, but it is as though Dostoevsky's Grand Inquisitor were cursing a placid Christ for His failure to address our real needs on earth. Unless he is dead, a man does not have the "liberty of lying like a stone," coiled in a state that requires no words to sustain it; to court that condition is to invite death's embrace. Pimber mistakenly saw Omensetter as the exception and tried to enter the enchanted, privileged circle, but Furber knows that innocence cannot stave off despair forever. "You're the one in luck," he announces to the dead Pimber, who is beyond the reach of language. Any living facsimile of transcendence, be it Furber's fortified garden or Omensetter's redoubtable luck, is a lie. But while Furber does not fall prey to illusion to the self-destructive extent that Pimber is he is not beyond wishing for permanent blindness: "Vision is no kindly injury" (p. 273).

Although Gass insists that art must convince us of its integrity apart from representational duties, the vitiated forms of art which rely upon unconditional withdrawal from a world which cannot measure up to the artist's aesthetic aspirations are shown to have a limited usefulness in *Omensetter's Luck*. Israbestis Tott's contraction into a fictionalized past becomes a prison of damaged perception; Pimber's messiah-making proves to be a fatal misapprehension; Omensetter's "artless" luck dissolves under inspection and, because it is based on obliviousness rather than insight, is at best a mixed blessing; Furber's isolation, which in contrast to Omensetter's natural state of being is manufactured with language, sanctions misanthropy and leaves Gilean's spiritual leader a spiteful, futile little man. None of these fictions invites emulation or participation because none of them promises the expansion of consciousness that Gass promotes. The two extremes characterized by the "philosophical" contrasts of Omensetter and Furber—the former encased in womb-like naiveté and the latter self-interred in a syntactical tomb—are unresponsive to the broad range of human needs; moreover, Omensetter's grace is inaccessible to post-lapsarian man, while Furber's verbal reality excludes human relationships in favor of linguistic ones. Finally, not even their exclusive proprietors benefit sufficiently from their fictions. Family illness plunges Omensetter into the mundane, despite the fact that he summons his luck as a child might cry for parents to take away his nightmare. Furber eventually chokes on the words that once nourished him, for, according to Keats, "The fancy cannot cheat so well as she is famed to do."[23] The realization of what his aesthetic has always lacked initiates Furber's nervous breakdown: "Listen, Furber said, when I was a little boy and learning letters—A . . . , B . . . , C . . . , love was never taught to me, I couldn't spell it, the 0 was always missing, or the V, so I wrote love like live, or lure, or late, or law, or liar" (p. 298).

Omensetter and his family leave Gilean, just barely escaping blame for Pimber's death and the tragedy of losing an infant son. Furber, too, is cancelled out by "a kind of joint pneumonia and madness" (p. 303) that leaves him a relic nobody notices anymore. It falls to Huffley, the new minister, to strike a harmony between Omensetter's and Furber's personalities and to supervise the convalescence of a town that wants to return to status quo. As a symbol of simple humanity—mediocre, perhaps, but possessing qualities of both body and spirit that accommodate the contradictory poles of human nature—Huffley exudes composure.[24] Apparently the townspeople automatically recognize his restorative abilities: "Lucky thing to get him, everybody said, a boy so near and squarely put together. He hoped to remodel; perhaps he'd add" (p. 303).

The reaction of Furber to his successor is particularly revealing. Despite Huffley's obvious shortcomings—notably, a limited vocabulary and an unimpressive imagination—this man does have a capacity Furber never did and one which he has only recently come to respect: the ability to engage in a community of feeling. From his sickbed, Furber is surprised to hear a "lusty voice" issue from Huffley's "narrow chest" (p. 304). Like Tott, Furber had been one to prefer flair over substance when men speak, but here was a preacher of ordinary verbal talents leading a "boisterous choir" toward God. (Furber's words, on the other hand, had only led to other words.) Instead of language creating an impasse, language is here a means of spiritual growth.

In short, words can fashion worlds which contain the fullness that is implied by the idea of "worlds." Ironically, it is the doggedly unspectacular Huffley who causes the cynical ex-preacher, who is awakened too late to the true wealth of words, to contribute the money found on Pimber's body (his "hanging money") to the church as his last, and only sincere, religious gesture.

3

In the Heart of the Heart of the Country:
Eyes Driven Back In

DESPITE THE AMBITION AND COMPLEXITY of *Omensetter's Luck,* William Gass's notoriety as a writer of fiction is typically attributed to his collection of short stories, *In the Heart of the Heart of the Country.* These stories appeared in 1968, two years after the publication of his novel. By Gass's own estimation, *In the Heart* contains much of his most successful writing to date; in addition, several of the stories— namely, the title piece, "The Pedersen Kid," and "The Order of Insects"—are among the most consistently anthologized works of recent "experimental" fiction, ranking Gass alongside John Barth, Donald Barthelme, and Robert Coover in terms of visibility on college syllabi.

Although each of the fictions in the collection was conceived as a separate entity, it profits us to read the collection as an integrated whole, as a series of variations on the theme of the pleasures and pitfalls of aesthetic isolation. From this vantage point, Jethro Furber, the dominant consciousness of *Omensetter's Luck,* can be seen as a precursor of the narrators presented in the stories. Each narrator is a mind in retreat, or, as the unnamed storyteller in the concluding story refers to himself, an eye driven inward; each hopes to secure a reliable refuge (resembling Furber's verbal architecture) that serves as an alternative to a world characterized as violent, tedious, loveless, or downright inscrutable.

Surely the environmental circumstances surrounding "The Pedersen Kid" seem to vindicate the flight of the narrator, young Jorge Segren, into the interior life. In contrast to Furber's thickly-worded garden, however, the words here barely emerge intact. Language is spare and brittle. Articulation, the definitive achievement of the fictional artist, withers against the frozen backdrop, where a ponderous silence rules.

Big Hans yelled, so I came out. The barn was dark, but the sun burned on the snow. Hans was carrying something from the crib. I yelled, but Big Hans didn't hear. He was in the house with what he had before I reached the steps.

It was the Pedersen Kid. Hans had put the kid on the kitchen table like you would a ham and started the kettle. He wasn't saying anything. I guess he figured one yell from the crib was enough noise. Ma was fumbling with the kid's clothes which were stiff with ice. She made a sound like whew from every breath. The kettle filled and Hans said,

Get some snow and call your pa.

Why?

Get some snow.[1]

The bleak landscape exerts a petrifying influence on the language generated there, and we might infer a metaphorical connection between the slow, ritualistic revival of the Pedersen Kid after his rescue from the snowstorm and Jorge's private establishment of consciousness and free will, which is described throughout the story in terms of a growing warmth inside him. As if to demonstrate Jorge's need to define himself apart from his environment, Gass reserves the lyrical passages of "The Pedersen Kid" for interior monologue— the sole context where beauty can develop uncontaminated.

Of the five stories in the collection, the first is the one most ostensibly indebted to the realistic tradition: conventions such as a powerfully realized setting, discreet characterization, and the familiar plot structure of a journey leading to some pivotal revelation are prominent components of "The Pedersen Kid." Relentlessly convoluted in design, as though the all-encompassing blizzard in the story were rendering all perception hesitant and indistinct, "The Pedersen Kid" is replete with allegorical options for the discerning reader and is equally accommodating to Freudian, Christian, and heraldic archetypes.[2] Nevertheless, these designs are merely scaffolds for the language they occasion. Despite Gass's surface adherence to the tenets of literary realism, according to which the tale takes priority over the technique, the shaping of a narrative detachment ultimately precedes the particulars of whatever "actually happened."[3]

As he did in *Omensetter's Luck,* Gass delves into a well-worn motif—a rite of initiation—to focus his symbolic analysis of the awakening of artistic temperament as exhibited by the unfolding of language. One dismal morning in North Dakota, Big Hans discovers the half-dead body of the Pedersen kid, a boy from a nearby farm, lying in the snow outside the Segren place. Once inside, Hans and Jorge return the frozen boy to consciousness with the aid of massage and Pa Segren's precious whiskey. The kid struggles to tell them that a stranger broke into his house and was holding his parents captive in the fruit cellar; the boy had managed to escape into the blizzard, but he feared that the menacing stranger had murdered his parents. After an argument with Jorge's brutish, alcoholic father, the three of them—Jorge, Pa, and Big Hans—

grudgingly board their wagon and head for the Pedersen place. Finding the stranger's frozen horse, Hans and Pa, whose mutual antagonism is apparent throughout the story, become temporary allies in the dubious project of tunneling through the snowdrift on the far side of the house as a surprise tactic. That effort proving useless, they advance to the barn, but they are reluctant to risk crossing the open space and entering the house. Jorge finally does so, but when his father follows, a gunshot drops him. The boy breaks through a basement window and huddles in anxious expectation of a confrontation with death. Curiously, the stranger never appears, and Jorge is left to contemplate his isolation, the presumed deaths of all the adults at the hands of the killer, and the sudden wellspring of joy he feels burning within him.

So goes the plot. But to be seduced by the naturalistic skin of the story into trying to burrow past the dense language in order to uncover the message buried beneath it is to discard the story's greater import, which has to do with the accumulation and patterning of the words themselves. Clearing away language so as to better view plot is self-defeating. Indeed, instead of illuminating the symbolic structure of the plot as the story progresses—a common aim of realistic fiction, in which perseverance is rewarded with the reliable dismantling of mystery—Gass steers us into cul-de-sacs, lets loose ends dangle, and plunges without warning into subjective distortions. Given his theoretical position that the verbal configuration itself (the pointing statue, rather than where it points) is the justification for fiction, we may well be to blame for our own misguided frustration. The identity of the yellow-gloved killer and the fates of the rest of the characters, both discoveries toward which the story seems to be directed, are not resolved; suspense is not relieved, as though the story purges itself of external distractions as it moves forward and refines out everything but the narrator's churning consciousness. Mental activity ultimately takes priority over the amenities of plot, and the central theme becomes the attempt to deliver oneself, if only psychologically, from the rigors of daily existence.

The dominant metaphors of heat and cold give continual evidence of this desire. Every character yearns to somehow create "spring inside": Big Hans secludes himself with his pictures of naked women; Pa fondles his whiskey bottle; his wife finds her solace in the maintenance of the household routine and in organizing her meager kitchen; and Jorge consoles himself with intricate dreams of prowess and liberation. Furthermore, these secret comforts provide the main source of self-worth for these characters. At times, for example, Pa displays a physical affection for his bottles—surely no person elicits such devoted feelings from him; paranoid about pilferage, he hides them about his property. "He took pride in his hiding," thinks Jorge, fearing his father's reaction to the fact that his mother had quickly rooted out a bottle for the failing Pedersen kid. "It was all the pride he had" (p. 8). Pride in hiding applies equally well to Jorge, who must always be alert to the incursions of hatred from his elders. He still recalls with pain and furor Pa's mutilation of his story book; it is a response very much in keeping with that of his father to the discovery of his own most precious possession. "I was cold in your house always, pa" (p. 74), the boy silently accuses, for the lack of intimacy and compassion there makes it little better than the wintry landscape outside.

No wonder that Jorge's immediate reaction to the arrival of the helpless Pedersen kid is one of resentment, for the frozen child commands center stage in a way Jorge, who regularly dodges physical abuse, never has. Jorge takes some satisfaction in having a larger penis than the competition, and he extends his hatred for Big Hans and Pa to young Pedersen;

whose dying supplants his own status in the Segren household: "I decided I hated the Pedersen kid too, dying in our kitchen while I was away where I couldn't watch, dying just to pleasure Hans and making me go up snapping steps and down a drafty hall" (p. 3). Pa smacks his son for waking him, and Jorge blames the Pedersen kid for that as well. In short, the appearance of the Pedersen kid emphasizes for Jorge his peripheral position. He has always been invisible because the adults around him are either incapable of or unwilling to see him; he predicts how his sodden father will blink at him "as if I were the sun off the snow and burning to blind him" (p. 3). Jorge targets his peer for scorn, boasting to himself that *he* would not have run if an intruder threatened his family, although in a house where he does not count, neither love nor duty seem appropriate motives for heroic sacrifice. Convinced that Pedersen's stupidity is the original cause of the kid's drinking his whiskey, Pa spews curses at him, and Jorge, in a rare display of solidarity, echoes his father's condemnations.

The decision to accept the Pedersen kid's tale results from complex and thoroughly self-centered impulses on the part of the "avengers." The fact that the warming operation performed by Big Hans is described in terms of kneading dough— the boy is resuscitated on the bread table, where he acquires a second skin of flour—is significant in the sense that the kid, as well as the plot he introduces, is being prepared for digestion. For what does "The Pedersen Kid"—the story and the human presence in the Segren kitchen—mean? Gass's characters are essentially faced with a malleable text, and they all take advantage of their opportunities to exercise subjective interests so as to develop a private understanding. Big Hans, Pa, and Jorge may be viewed at this point as fiction-makers, not just as an audience for the Pedersen kid. Bringing the boy to consciousness is, in addition to an act of restoration, an act of creation; it imitates Gass's construction of the text and our efforts to recapitulate and evaluate the ambiguous material before us.

Therefore, the identity of the yellow-gloved intruder, initially obscured by the Pedersen kid's fear, is buried deeper and deeper by the various prejudices of his potential benefactors. Such is Gass's layering technique: "The problem is to present evil as a visitation—sudden, mysterious, violent, inexplicable. All should be subordinated to that end. The physical representation must be spare and staccato; the mental representation must be flowing and a bit repetitious; the dialogue realistic but musical. A ritual effect is needed."[4] Accordingly, the preternatural incarnation and menacing silence of the killer steep him in a mist of unreality; he is the abominable snowman, winter's harshness in human form.

Hans is alone in accepting the kid's story without qualification, perhaps because, having been the instrument of his salvation, Hans is compelled to unite his version of reality with the one proposed by the kid. Jorge recognizes Hans's perturbation when Pa insists that the kid was simply making the whole thing up to excuse his "fool stunt" of running off into a snowstorm: "Hans didn't like that. He didn't want to believe the kid any more than I did, but if he didn't then the kid had fooled him sure. He didn't want to believe that either" (p. 17). To his chagrin, Hans realizes that the truth he advocates requires him to follow through, to go to the Pedersen house and face the danger waiting there—a terrifying consequence with which Jorge delights in plaguing Hans. The kid lives for Hans and because of Hans's attention, which thereby requires him to acknowledge the killer's reality as well: "Rubbing. You didn't know what you were bringing to, did you? Something besides the kid came through the storm,

Hans" (p. 22). So Hans grimly takes on the challenge to his pride. As for Pa, his motive for joining the expedition is to release his wrath (his own pride having been damaged by the discovery of his hidden whiskey) in the form of leering disdain for Hans.

Jorge has no personal stake in this plan at first. His Pedersen kid is dead, so the story the kid gives is negligible. Instead, Jorge is bullied into the plot by the men. (Free will must be supported by physical might in order to be respected by men like Pa and Hans.) But almost imperceptibly, Jorge's attitude toward the Pedersen kid changes as the plot unfolds. Competition slowly turns to emulation. Jorge imagines that the crawling coldness he feels in the snow matches the sensation that must have crept over the Pedersen kid earlier. Furthermore, in reversing the kid's journey, Jorge figures to reverse his fortune; he welcomes the chance to prove himself better than the kid in a crisis:

It was like I was setting out to do something special and big—like a knight setting out—worth remembering. I dreamed coming from the barn and finding his back to me in the kitchen and wrestling with him and pulling him down and beating the stocking cap off his head with the barrel of the gun. I dreamed coming in from the barn still blinking with the light and seeing him there and picking the shovel up and taking him on. That had been then, when I was warm, when I was doing something big, heroic even, and well worth remembering. I couldn't put the feeling down in Pedersen's back yard or Pedersen's porch or barn. I couldn't see myself, or going slowly up and down in ma's face and ma shooing it away and at the same time trying not to move an inch for getting shot (pp. 32–33).

Beyond Jorge's wish to save his family, of course, is the desire to endanger them in the first place. Ultimately, Jorge embraces the shadowy killer who shoots his father as an embodiment of vengeance for years of mistreatment; he is the instrument by which Jorge seizes the role of protagonist in his own life. In the end, warming in the Pedersen basement, he muses about the possibility that Hans and Ma are also dead now, which would grant him by default the prominence he seeks.

There is, of course, the reality beyond artistic manipulation to be considered: the hard journey through the snow, the dead horse in the snowdrift, and finally, the unavoidable presence of the killer himself. All of these details are incontrovertible; their weirdness or unpleasantness resists redefinition. They all require that the kid's story be credited. The tiny peculiarity of the killer's yellow gloves is enough to initiate a feeling of being caught up in a reality that overmatches the fictionalizing impulse: "It's like something you see once and it hits you so hard you never forget it even if you want to; lies, dreams, pass—this *has* you; it's like something that sticks to you like burrs, burrs you try to brush off while you're doing something else, but they never brush off, they just roll a little, and the first thing you know you ain't doing what you set out to, you're just trying to get them burrs off" (p. 17). Inexplicably, but beyond doubt, there is the killer, and asking how or why he'd come through the blizzard to assault the Pedersens cannot remove that "burr": "He was in it now and he could go on and he could come through it because he had before. Maybe he belonged in the snow. Maybe he lived there, like a fish does in a lake. Spring didn't have anything like him" (p. 72). There is no mistaking the admiration which overshadows Jorge's fear at this moment. Later, from the confines of the Pedersen cellar, Jorge will be able to fashion a truce with the cold, his life-long symbolic adversary, because it has struck Pa and Big Hans down.

Jorge's inner warmth—the physical manifestation of an energized consciousness—develops only after the trial by winter. Pitted against the cold are a series of images of wombs, tunnels, and shelters which serve as psychological attempts to marshal his waning resources. Unfortunately, memories of warmth are evanescent: "I tried to hold the feeling but it was warm as new bath water and just as hard to hold" (p. 32). The cold, however, is always present, and its main effect on Jorge is to paralyze his imagination, to confront him with his enslavement to insensitive men, and thus, to stir him to helpless rage. Forced out of the wagon to stab about in the snow for the bottle his father dropped, Jorge consoles and fortifies himself with dreams of vengeance: "It was frightening—the endless white space. I'd have to keep my head down. Winded slopes and rises all around me. I'd never wanted to go to Pedersen's. That was Hans's fight, and Pa's. I was just cold . . . cold . . . and scared and sick of snow. That's what I'd do if I found it—kick it under a drift" (p. 39). His hatred intensifies, pervading the scene like the weather. Treated as an appendage in the employ of adults who show greater affection for horses and inanimate possessions than they do for Jorge, he suspects the cold of having conspired with his enemies, since it seems as if the cold, like Pa's wrath and Hans's sullenness, is directed against him personally. In spite of concentrating on an image of a kettle steaming on the stove, Jorge cannot neglect for long the sense of his "breath coming slow and cloudy and hanging heavy and dead in the still air" (p. 43).

To counter his environmental and human oppressors, Jorge envisions the pleasures of sanctuary, which his alter ego, the Pedersen kid, has already attained by having made his way through the snow. Ironically, the snow itself tantalizes him with this very promise. The makeshift tunnel, which turns out to be useless as a means of approaching the Pedersen house, does have the psychological appeal of being a barrier against the elements: "It would have been wonderful to burrow down, disappear under the snow, sleep out of the wind in soft sheets, safe" (p. 57). In fact, throughout the story, the snow's opposing connotations wage war in Jorge's mind: it is both hazard and refuge; its coldness burns.

This paradoxical linkage particularly asserts itself after Jorge, partly to show his bravery and partly to escape the domination of the men, challenges the vast open space and makes it into the cellar. The symbolic circuit between the Pedersen kid and Jorge Segren, who has retraced and mirrored the kid's adventure, is complete, and the narrator, along with his imaginative sensibilities, begins to thaw out. From his fetal position in a dark, moldy corner, fantasies are released from deep freeze: "But I stayed where I was, so cold I seemed apart from myself, and wondered if everything had been working to get me in this cellar as a trade for the kid he'd missed. Well, he was sudden. The Pedersen kid—maybe he'd been a message of some sort. No, I liked better the idea that we'd been prisoners exchanged. I was back in my own country. A new blank land. More and more, while we'd been coming, I'd been slipping out of myself, pushed out by the cold maybe . . . . Suppose the snow was a hundred feet deep. Down and down. A blue-white cave, the blue darkening. Then tunnels off of it like the branches of trees. And fine rooms. Was it February by now?" (pp. 62–63) Note the concept of "a new blank land," a profound contrast to the sensation of fear that Jorge felt outside from "the space that was bowling up inside me, a white blank glittering waste like the waste outside, coldly burning" (p. 45). What had earlier been the white of bleakness and despair is transformed into the white of unbridled possibility—the artist's open canvas awaiting his unique imprint.

Despite the looming danger of an unseen killer—and were the dead bodies of the Pedersens behind the next door?—Jorge settles into the rare ease of nostalgia. He recalls an idyllic summer when he roamed carefree over the plain, pretending to shoot any unwitting passersby with a broomstick. He was enjoying the game of ascendancy over his father (one of the "shooting" victims), the liberty it afforded, and the sensual pleasures of a warm, bright day; it would be "a special shame" to forego this satisfaction "on the edge of something wonderful" (p. 65) to return to the snow and his father's snarling commands. That peaceful summer, he realizes, was the last time he felt so free, until now; when the summer ended, winter and the mutual antagonism of Pa and Hans set in. Jorge also remembers Pa's desecration of a favorite picture book, whose pieces the vicious man scattered in the privy; having once emptied the contents of his chamberpot on Hans, Pa is regularly associated with excrement in Jorge's mind, and he is initially described while he is sleeping as "dung covered with snow" (p. 3). Why go back to that, now that his own body seems a new, intriguing territory to be explored? How can Jorge surrender his refuge, now that the cellar air is suddenly sweet?

How hospitable of the killer to free him from that responsibility! Jorge's "proposal" that the killer visit the Segren house—ostensibly to provide a test of Jorge's mettle, but also to relieve him of the stifling authority of adults, as the killer had already done for the Pedersen kid—comes true in his mind after the actual shooting of Pa. However, as the storyline frays into uncertainty, the circumstances of Pa's death cloud over: perhaps it is Jorge himself who shoots his father, fulfilling the wish he had intimated in his summer reverie, while the yellow-gloved man stands as a needed screen to protect him from the awful guilt.[5] "The kid for killing his family must freeze" (p. 66) is one uninvited thought that darkens Jorge's celebration of awakening selfhood. Indeed, Jorge may be freezing to death, and doubt thereby veils the entire closing section of his narrative. It remains questionable whether the "melting away" of the threats that surround him in this strange seclusion is a delusion; what is most definite about the final paragraph of "The Pedersen Kid," of course, is Jorge's alliance with the "heroic" stranger: "I had been the brave one and now I was free. The snow would keep me. I would bury pa and the Pedersens and Hans and even ma if I wanted to bother. I hadn't wanted to come but now I didn't mind. The kid and me, we'd done brave things well worth remembering. The way that fellow had come so mysteriously through the snow and done us such a glorious turn— well it made me think how I was told to feel in church. The winter time had finally got them all, and I really did hope that the kid was as warm as I was now, warm inside and out, with joy" (pp. 78–79).

Jorge manages to create and interpret the plot that contains him; that is the nature of his heroism. He seizes destiny imaginatively, and that is the wellspring of power. (He can even choose which of the other characters he'll bury!) Speaking of the fiction of Borges, Gass declares, "Any metaphor which is taken with literal seriousness requires us to imagine a world in which in can be true; it contains or suggests a metaphorical principle that in turn gives form to a fable."[6] Although he has Borges' fictions in mind, the procedure Gass outlines applies to Jorge Segren's method as well. By preferring the realm of metaphor over physical environment, Jorge creates a surrogate world, in which his own aspirations can be attained and are the dominant, actual ones.

Instead of advancing an alternative world, the untamed narrator of "Mrs. Mean" uses language to suspend himself "upon a web of theory—as ready as the spider is to mend or suck dry intruders."[7] His repudiation of the external world is interrupted by his fascination with its particulars, especially its sexual overtones. In a manner reminiscent of Jethro Furber's, he observes from a voyeuristic abeyance the ordinary inhabitants of his neighborhood, who are rendered mysterious by the deliberate distance that the narrator maintains from them.

The plot as such is the unfolding of a consciousness obsessed by the tension between approach and avoidance. "Mrs. Mean" is actually an elaborate depiction of the limbo state which the worship of language over life can foster. Gass's assessment of the language which fills Donald Barthelme's stories is applicable here: constrained to types, human relationships are superficial, and words evolving from them "produce an appearance of communion, the illusion of knowledge. Counterfeit, they purchase jail."[8]

Accordingly, the narrator of "Mrs. Mean" supplants the world with a private reality whose rules and definitions place him in control. "I call her Mrs. Mean" (p. 80), begins his fiction, but he admits quite readily that he does not know her name; the point is that he has not granted her the privilege of asserting her own reality. Instead, he authors her with the self-proclaimed impunity of a novelist wording his characters. (The recklessness of treating people as though they were just ficitonal characters has already been shown in conjunction with Furber's "creation" of Omensetter, and the same dangers are evident in this story.) Reducing the woman to "the grotesqueries of type" (p. 80), he hopes to ensure his relative superiority over his neighborhood, which seems to him bland and desolate. Due to the stranglehold his consciousness maintains over the environment, however, we quickly suspect that all the information we receive in "Mrs. Mean" is colored by the narrator's urge toward dominion, and that the decay he reports may perhaps be in part a projection of a self mouldering in its solipsistic prison. But while he commends himself for his "scientific" detachment—other people are organisms whose activities and responses to stimuli are to be watched with disinterest and dutifully recorded—he cannot entirely sanction his own coldness: "I take their souls away— I know it—and I play with them; I puppet them up to something; I march them through strange crowds and passions; I snuffle at their roots" (p. 83). This process smacks of vulgarity. In contrast to the daily rounds of gossip (that great distributor of mutual confidence) practiced by Mrs. Mean and Mrs. Cramm, the narrator's interests are exploitative and calculated to gain advantage over more primitive life forms. He lays his fictions upon the population and imagines himself supernatural, dreadful in their eyes (p. 84).

In fact, the narrator is also a victim of psychological necessity. Distance and control are the interdependent factors that protect his "budding world," which would be demolished were the puppets free inside of it (p. 87). He further justifies this tyranny by convincing himself that all encounters are a case of devour-or-be-devoured, thereby illustrating the dictum that untrustworthy people trust no one's intentions.

Although it becomes clear that Mrs. Mean's threat is concerned primarily with sexual intimidation, the narrator revises the affront on the conscious level to the crime of child abuse. Once again, despite his impatience with her four incorrigible children and her use of physical punishment and public humiliation as means of keeping them in line, there is nothing so very unique or outrageous in her behavior; Mrs. Mean is the narrator's invention. The narrator's version makes her a fairy-tale witch and her children innocent victims. And his imposed organization brooks no questioning, either. He casually dismisses his wife's suggestion that Mrs. Mean might have a more tender side which she displays inside her house—how could the children so passively sacrifice themselves by entering the monster's lair? He himself is troubled by the obvious nastiness and stupidity of the children to whom he tries to assign sympathetic roles in his fiction. But eventually he is able to reinforce his stereotypes against contradiction: "Of course that singleness of sight has always been my special genius" (p. 109). Other neutral characteristics—her preoccupation with her lawn, her unflinching heartiness, her external occupation—are insulting to the supremely idle narrator. Because she is in so many ways his opposite, he feels he must attack her in order to validate himself.

And yet, unlike the other people he spies upon, Mrs. Mean defies the narrator's attempts to bend her to his imagination: "Except in the case of Mrs. Mean. I am no representative of preternatural power. I am no image, on my porch— no symbol. I don't exist. However I try, I cannot, like the earth, throw out invisible lines to trap her instincts; turn her north or south; fertilize or not her busy womb; cause her to exhibit the tenderness, even, of ruthless wild things for her wild and ruthless brood. And so she burns and burns before me. She revolves her backside carefully against a tree" (p. 88). Everything about her (though most importantly, the sexual trepidation she triggers) disrupts his composure and conviction of superiority. She is simply too strong a challenge for his manipulations. Overwhelming the effort to stereotype

her into submission, Mrs. Mean withstands imaginative forays as though she were "impenetrable jelly" (p. 89). The self-
appointed "God of idleness" resorts to the dream that she
will be felled by a cramp during her lawnwork and suffer "the
blaze of God in her eye" (p. 89), but the desire merely
shames him with his impotence. Consequently, the narrator
elects to work on Mr. Wallace as a sort of tune-up bout for a
tougher adversary.

Poor Mr. Wallace only desires a little conversation. As it
happens, he has nothing but his catalogue of aches to offer,
and in the confines of his narrow interests the narrator feels
suffocated. Nevertheless, for all his infirmities, Wallace lives;
the narrator notes the old man's great belly, which we may
take as both a symbol of his appetite for experience (as opposed to the narrator's conditional relationship to the world)
and as a sign that he might "swallow" the narrator, which is
to say that the trapper feels threatened by entrapment. When
Wallace sides with the enemy by treasonously visiting the
Means, the narrator strips him of his freedom. He convinces
Wallace of the magical properties of moles and coaxes him
into confessing the nature and location of his wife's blemishes. Given the sexual fetishism of the narrator, this is no
random choice of punishment: "Even now I dare not let my
mind look upon the picture of that pair peering beneath her
lifted skirts. How infernally lewd! How majestically revolt-
ing!" (p. 112) The triumph is assured when the narrator off-
handedly discredits the significance of moles at the height of
Wallace's enslavement to their mystery.

Still, it's a paltry show of power, and its rewards are short-
lived. Mrs. Mean still looms; her house is a bulwark of ambiguity. While the narrator's wife is content to let her interest in
the neighbors stop at the Means's door, he cannot be so casual,

and tries to create what he cannot perceive. He musters his faculties against the blockade, loath to succumb to his wife's failure of imagination:

I, on the other hand, cut surgically by all outward growths, all manifestations, merely, of disease and reach the ill within. I conceive the light, for instance, as always bad, of insufficient strength and a poor color, as having had to travel through too much dust and too much muslin, as having had to dwell too long in the company of dark rugs and mohair chairs and satin-shaded lamps. The air, I feel, is bad too. The windows never open. The back door bangs but the breeze is metaphorical. All things in their little house that hang, hang motionless and straight. Nothing is dirty, but nothing feels clean. Their writing paper sticks to the hand. Their toilet sweats. The halls are cool. The walls are damp (p. 104).

Surely tidiness is impossible inside that house. Inevitably, the narrator envisions an interior that exudes the same half-seductive, half-nauseating sexuality that its shadowy inhabitant herself suggests; he associates this complex set of responses with the mixture of disgust and wonder he once felt when, as a child playing near the family porch, he suddenly discovered fat, white slugs. This association is consistent with his typical reduction of members of the Mean family to animals, such as vermin, toads, and "fly-beleaguered bears," as if, diminished, they might be more manageable.

The story reaches its climax when the narrator begins to disown his life-at-a-remove and transgresses the antiseptic mental world in favor of direct contact with the world he has been spying upon.[9] Abstract imaginings and a screen of words have not nourished him enough.[10] There must be "sweet times," he thinks, which "lie beyond my conjuring" (p. 113). Aesthetic limitations now define the inadequacy of this artist's isolation of and in the mind; the consolation of having superimposed a model of verbal organization over most of his environment does not eliminate the massive, formidable portion of the outside world that will not submit to story.

The narrator cannot encompass the Means without jeopardizing his trascendent state, and he does exceed the norm among Gass's artists in piercing his obstructive fictions in order to confront the characters with greater immediacy. One night he stalks the house, hoping to eavesdrop on the hidden passions of his neighbors, but he is acutely aware of the foolishness and meagerness of his actions. Feeling vulnerable in the empty alley, he finds that he has only succeeded in tunneling further into private fantasies; "I realize that I have breached the fortress, yet in doing so I lost all feeling for the Means and sensed only myself, fearful, hiding from a child. . . . Indeed I am not myself. This is not the world. I have gone too far. It is the way fairy tales begin—with a sudden slip over the rim of reality" (p. 117). Long devotion to self-contained art has made him a victim of the very abstractions he has manufactured. For him, reality as such has ceased to exist because, as he discovers to his dismay, it is inaccessible. Ducking about the backside of the house, stealing into the garage, the narrator relinquishes his former illusion of majesty. The God of idleness is in the end a furtive Peeping Tom who is plagued by the poverty of the withdrawal for which he has settled. His closing complaint announces his frustration and may serve as a warning to Gass's entire collection of artists who trade life for language:

I am terribly and recklessly impelled to force an entrance to their lives, the lives of all of them; even, although this is absurd, to go into the fabric of their days, to mote the air with my eyes and move with their pulse and share their feelings; to be the clothes that lie against their skins, to shift with them, absorb their smells. Oh I know the thought is awful, yet I do not care. To have her anger bite and burn inside me, to have his brute lust rise in me at the sight of her sagging, tumbling breasts, to meet her flesh and his in mine or have the sores of Mr. Wallace break my skin or the raw hoot of his wife crawl out my throat . . . I do not care . . . I do not care. The desire is as strong as any I have ever had: to see, to feel, to know, and to possess! Shut in my room as I so often am now with my wife's eyes fastened to the other side of the door like blemishes in the wood, I try to analyze my feelings. I lay them out one by one like fortune's cards and clothes for journeying and when I see them clearly then I know the time is only days before I shall squeeze through the back screen of the Means' house and be inside (pp. 118–19).

No matter how misleading the temptations of retreat into private artifice may turn out to be in Gass's fiction, it is easy to understand why the artist figures discussed so far are eager to succumb. Whatever their drawbacks, each of the alternative realities offer beauty, coherence, reliability, and the illusion of personal prowess and command over one's surroundings. Even though faith in the imagination often proves premature, the belief in that faith as a last-ditch reconnaissance mission of consciousness is something with which any reader who is disappointed or repulsed by real-world circumstances can identify. The development of a controlling perspective, the restoration of foiled sensibilities, and the gap between what ought to be and what actually is the nature of life in the contemporary world all serve to justify, at least in the mind of the character who is desperate for such justification, the fiction that may save him from capitulation.

But what sets "Icicles" apart from the thematic strain which Gass has previously constructed is the transparent insufficiency of the fictional refuge from the point of view of the fiction-maker himself, as though the meagerness of the external world were a force capable of infiltrating consciousness so thoroughly that no imaginative compensation is free from its debilitating effects. Charlie Fender is doomed both by a de-humanizing daily routine and by the fragility of the artwork in which he hopes to enclose himself. Having neither the brute aptitude of those who can contend with the world on its own terms, nor the creative resources necessary to compose a viable alternative, Fender founders helplessly, perpetually retreating without the encouragement of a firm destination.

Icicles provide Gass with one of his most multifarious symbols, not all of whose connotations are soothing. Pure and gleaming as the sun blazing on the snow in "The Pedersen Kid," they do not enchant Fender at first. There is also something diabolical about the way they curtain his house; the shards threaten like teeth framing the mouth of a cave or, as befits Fender's regressive nature, a dentated portal to a womb.

As his name implies, Fender does not act so much as react, deflecting the incursions of other people. Unfortunately, this particular solitude is furnished by an artist of limited talents: "He hated winter. The same gray sky lay on the ground, day after day, gray as industrial smoke, and in the sky the ground floated like a street that's been salted, and his closets were cold, holes wore through his pockets, and he was lonely, indoors and out, with a loneliness like the loneliness of overshoes or someone else's cough."[11] The blatant irony of a real estate salesman, a man whose livelihood depends upon accosting people, cowering from his clients is but one aspect of Fender's affliction. (Overwhelmed at times by the tawdriness of his job—so calculating, so full of double-dealing—he has to restrain himself from dissuading the clients he is supposed to be selling.) Worse is the fact that his detachment is not transcendence, but sheer alienation. He does not even enjoy a sense of authority over his own restricted space: scorching his tongue during dinner, he vaguely considers cooling it against his windowpane, but because the strange act might not be condoned in public, he cannot dare it privately either (pp. 122–23). In short, he is a vagrant wherever he goes, and he feels his house is vacant even while he inhabits the premises; like Eliot's Gerontion, that "dull head among windy spaces,"[12] Fender despairs because he lacks redemptive contacts and suffers a nagging feeling of uncertain tenancy.

Fender's co-workers intensify his discomfort by emphasizing a doctrine that reduces people to objects. There is Glick, a younger employee who advises Charlie and outstrips his senior mainly because of his unflappable self-absorption. Glick reminds Fender of those icy shards: his eyes seem to stick into their objectives, and his manner consistently unnerves Fender, who finds the man to be "a bramble, a burr" (p. 138), and an incessant bother. More to the point, Glick is a rival for the attentions of Isabelle, and the competition goes badly for Fender: while she and Glick bandy puns and he impresses her with flourishes of Latin when describing his passion for botany, Fender just broods and worries that he is the butt of some incomprehensible joke. While the younger man outwords him, Fender silently plans to write a pot pie manufacturer about the false promise regarding the number of chunks of beef he could expect to find in his meal. A prodigious pickle in Fender's mind (p. 122), Glick absently displays his potency and threatens Fender's: he is a man given to tearing the heads off flowers and kicking the icicles off car bumpers. Fender, on the other hand, is a man whom the census neglects and who cannot recall his own life story; he plots to plunge an icicle (the ideal murder weapon, for it disappears after the crime) into grinning Glick's chest.

Of course, such schemes illustrate Fender's ineffectuality. He generally quails before stronger personalities. Whereas other salesmen calmly assess and "go with the flow," Fender is convinced that he is just a loose stick at the mercy of a river's current (p. 139). Bereft of the stable footholds in reality which others seem to come by naturally, he describes himself as "a man without a place to be, a place that's known, that has a name, is some way fixed; why that's like being alone at sea without a log to hang on—and the sharks at your toes. Fender shrugged. Fender: you have no job. You lack an occupation. Fender—a position. Fender—a spot to johnny on. He shrugged. Yeah. He lacked. And Fender—Charlie Fender— of such and such a number, such and such a road, in such and such a town and state, has quit, is fired, is out, at his age, after so, so many years. . . . Yes, he thought, I do not even occupy myself" (p. 157).

Chief among those who would instruct Fender in the strenuous way of the world is Mr. Pearson, the boss and unexcelled purveyor of crassness. Pearson is reminiscent of several of Stanley Elkin's characters in that he is a vocation endowed with a voice and liberated from conventional restraints. Try as Fender may to parry his influence, Pearson "pierces" the feeble psychological defenses available to the beleaguered salesman.[13]

Pearson praises the profession that so troubles Fender as one might praise a lover; he is married to the job with the exclusiveness we would expect from someone "being married to the church. Like nuns or monks are" (p. 124). He preaches a diabolical manifesto, according to which, property is exalted— real estate is the *real* estate—and human beings are demoted to the status of merchandise. More bully than mentor—Pearson's spiel gives Fender "an earful of ice" (p. 124)—Pearson is still irresistible, showering the same practiced bombast on his employee that buoys his own pride. Convinced that realtors are the Fates of the community, he revels in his "mission," which is to take action to define the cutting edge of progress: "Fender, the thing is: it's moving, and the thing to ask yourself is: am I going to create, control, direct, manage, *make* that move, or is it going to manage and move and make me? see?" (p. 129) Pearson infuses the landscape with his juggernautical ego; he makes rules with the arrogance of a contemporary deity.

The cornerstone of Pearson's philosophy is the equation of people and things. Human bodies are properties, Pearson explains, as he inspects Isabelle's earlobe with inky fingers. (Meanwhile, of course, Fender crouches inside himself like a crustacean within its shell, or like the peas in the pot pies he complains about, and he imagines himself having to hoist himself up to his eyeholes to look out.) By Pearson's logic, the reality of property subdues any other. Our possessions possess us: "Listen: *property owns people.* Everything's property, and the property that lasts longest—it owns what lasts least. Stands to reason. Fender, Fender, wait'll you die, you'll see! So the property that lives, Fender, that lasts and lives and goes right on, Fender, and then goes on again, that overlives us, Fender, that *overlives* . . . well, that's the property that's real, and *it—it owns the rest*—lock, stock, and barrel—*right?* Makes sense" (p. 131).

The consequences of this dictate include the disqualification of Fender's refuge. In "Philosophy and the Form of Fiction," Gass establishes a precedent for the usurpation of consciousness that Pearson achieves over Fender. He delineates in this essay the strange alchemy through which the novelist makes the familiar world of the reader strange; for instance, Samuel Beckett strips away his riches and sweeps aside his preconceptions, supplanting them with "a burlap bag, unopened tins, dirty thoughts, and webby privates."[14] The reader loses track of the old certainties and is taught to dance with shadows. Endlessly available to deception, Gass holds in awe those writers through whom "I can learn to hate my pleasures, condemn my desires, doubt my motives, deny my eyes, put unseen creatures in the world and then treat them with greater reverence, give them greater powers than those I innocently know—to bow and bow and bow in their direction; I can replace love for people with a love for principle, and even pursue a life beyond the grave as a program for the proper pursuit of this one. Bravo, novelists and philosophers; good show."[15] Fender's reality is similarly readjusted, though hardly with splendid results. Pearson bewitches his salesman, planting him in an atmosphere of cheap sloganism. "Since there is no out-of-doors in the world where language is the land,"[16] Fender is essentially condemned to a strict design, like a character pressed between the covers of a book, without privileges of negotiation.

Once the imagination is plundered and consciousness is overrun, one no longer controls his own fictions, much less the outside world; and since Gass suspects "that madness is a fiction lived in like a rented room,"[17] we might diagnose Fender's state of mind accordingly. Chair arms threaten to "enwooden" him (p. 157). The contours of his house confine him in a stiff second skin: "His little house possessed him, it was true. He'd been cut to fit its walls. He saw what it permitted. He did not reach beyond the rooms" (p. 131). The predicament becomes clearer still when Gass reveals that the relationship between physical and psychological constriction was the initial intrigue of his title metaphor: "Icicles once dripped solidly from my eaves, for instance. I thought them remarkable because they seemed to grow as a consequence of their own grief, and I wondered whether my feelings would freeze to me by the time they had traveled my length, and whether each of us wasn't just the size of our consciousness solidified."[18]

An imagination stuck in the skull promises little. Although Fender tells himself that it is preferable "to live like a mole out of eyeshot" (p. 135) rather than ally himself with the likes of Glick and Pearson, it is a feeble consolation indeed that he smuggles into his hole, where spontaneity is exchanged for ritual and intrepidness for indirection. Even more distressing to the character who sells out for sanctuary is the possibility that, because the person has been so thoroughly infiltrated, the creations of the self, though they may stem from antagonistic reactions to an oppressive environment, may actually be expressions of that environment at the same time. One may be a prisoner of his context to the extent that the individual will become an anachronism. Charles Russell argues that the tension between private and collective domains—the desire to establish a subjective presence that is stable enough to be reliable, yet protean enough to escape collaboration with a static, deadening society—is at the heart of postmodern culture. In the literature under discussion, Gass takes on the problem and bequeaths it to his fictional artists.

Both writer and character realize that successful self-definition depends on developing techniques of constant testing and interpreting of self and the encroaching world. They devise strategies of retreat or antagonism, of formalism or disruption. But since the integrity of personal identity is ever in doubt and the nature of the threatening environment is rarely revealed, these figures are never sure whether such disruption and creation prove to be adequate responses. Self-reflexive creative freedom may be but an expression of social encapsulation; disruption of the environment or text may result in a debilitating fragmentation of self or voice; and instead of providing an understanding of the social context, individual liberation may only unveil the visionary dreams and destructive reality of anarchism.[19]

Fender finds his creative outlets reduced to mere interior decorating. The chance to transmit the growing significance of the icicles to his own situation briefly arises. He comes to admire the icicles' phallic grandeur. (He considers taking stock of his pride with a tape measure!) Moreover, he intuitively realizes a kinship between the beauty of the icicles and the hidden potential of their "possessor," thus managing to temporarily disregard his boss's reversal of that hierarchy between owner and owned (according to which we might just as well interpret the icicles as fixing Fender behind some sort of cryogenic seal). Why could they not signal nature's favor after all, like any other physical attribute? "Only the icicles mattered . . . . If he could grow them inside himself, if he could swallow them like a carnival performer and put their beauty in his body" (p. 155). Fender's musing trails off here, but the implication is clear: he envisions a transubstantiation, a glimmering possibility of rebirth.

As beauty resolves itself as the dominant feature of the icicles, Fender unites them in his mind with the inaccessible Isabelle. This is the apex of his ingenuity: "He would frequently rest to watch his icicles, the whole line, firing up, holding to the sun like a maiden in her sleep or a princess in her tower— so real, so false, so magical. It was his own invention, that image, and he was proud of it" (p. 154). But before long, structural damage inherent in the fiction, like flaws in the ice, split his satisfaction apart. If icicles are pure, radiant, and self-perpetuating, they are also fragile and unresilient. No matter how tenaciously Fender may commit his already dubious energies to defending the icicles, there are always reckless children or thoughtless passersby who will outflank him and bring them crashing down. Nature itself threatens to dissolve its own casual creation, for sun and wind are indomitable enemies. Fender watches the mailman brush by and is terrified; he sees the child of prospective buyers cradling a huge icicle that he has snapped from the side of the house they are considering and, sharing in the house's injury, he drives the family away with his incomprehensible rage. Realizing, mournfully, that winter's beauty will eventually perish, Fender feels deceived, abused.

"Icicles" concludes with Fender's realization that he faces a profound dilemma: having repudiated the world in favor of his uniquely sheltered aesthetic, he must deal with its evanescence. Therefore, neither the intimacy of company nor the redemption of an artfully furnished solitude can be counted on. Fender ends as he began, in loneliness, but is now a loneliness unfortified by the illusion of transcendence: "The wall went into the ceiling at the wall's fold. He gave his head a crank to follow; saw the ceiling: gray white similarities of space, quite grayish, sunless, not about to snow, undappled, white, weighted, heaven, up and down, so far, so low, his whole height, lengthy, heavy as a purchase—the same unsagging same. Listen, I'm trying to tell you, Fender. We all come to it. That's the way it goes. It's simple. You got a place and nobody wants to live in it" (p. 161). A vulnerable shut-in braces against an avalanche of noisy children, who seem to be plummeting down upon him "like a snowfall of rocks" (p. 162). We suspect, however, that burying the defenseless Fender alive in his fortress-turned-crypt is simply redundant at this point.

"The Order of Insects" is the shortest work in *In the Heart,* and it dramatizes in miniature the critical instant when consciousness is first arrested by structure. In fact, the drawbacks of artifice which compromise its attractiveness in Gass's other works are not so apparent in this story; whereas the various refuges inhabited by Furber, Fender, and the others are often seen as reductive, stifling, or unwholesome, the order which beckons the unnamed female narrator of "The Order of Insects" is beautiful, even majestic, despite its being manifested as carcasses of bugs.

José Ortega y Gasset, a prominent touchstone in Gass's criticism, provides the term "infrarealism" to define fiction that focuses on what usually escapes notice.[20] In this story, a woman is confronted with the ineluctable "thereness" of highly organized microstructures that seem to signify the natural existence of the coherence which Gass's artists try to produce synthetically.

The choice of a woman protagonist for the story is particularly important. The drabness of life, a decisive impetus for several characters of artistic temperament who opt for imaginative alternatives that promise to be more conducive to their sensibilities, is in her case intensified by having been programmed into the confining stereotype of the housewife. Not only her daily activities, but also her emotional and intellectual responses to her environment are so routine that she is incapable at the beginning of the story of acknowledging profounder experiences than those traditionally associated with her limited role. Clearly, she has learned to evade potential disturbances by retreating into a tightly circumscribed self-concept: she prides herself on the fastidious way she goes about her housework, carefully sealing out the dirt and organizing the cupboards. As a woman, she is privileged, or forced, to edit out intrigue. Time and again her incipient fascination with the insects is hampered by the suspicion that the subject is too indelicate for the weaker sex: "It's no study for a woman . . . bugs,"[21] she reasons, and she later worries that the growing revelation she allows herself is something no woman is worthy of (p. 171).

Appreciating the order of insects, then, requires a broadening of the self—a significant change from the contractions of self which so frequently prove to be the price of withdrawal in Gass's fictions. The woman is actually thrust into a limbo between the mundane, "appropriate" affairs and the superior order of "the dark soul of the world itself" (p. 168).

That her earlier order was just a kind of incarceration is evidenced by the superficiality of the artistry it enables her to practice and by the automatic way she recoils from strange encounters. She is, quite literally, wife of the house, relegated to pettiness. Even her fears are ordinary: "Womanly, wifely, motherly ones: the children may point at the wretch with the hunch and speak in a voice he will hear; the cat has fleas again, they will get in the sofa; one's face looks smeared, it's because of the heat; is the burner under the beans? the washing machine's obscure disease may reoccur, it rumbles on rinse and rattles on wash; my god it's already eleven o'clock; which one of you has lost a galosh?" (p. 168) Mired in this relentlessly unpoetic state of mind, she has only revulsion for the tiny corpses which have infiltrated her home, as mysteriously and inexorably as they will soon invade her consciousness. (For had not a similar episode of pestilence driven her family to move out of one house—"after all we had been through in the other place," she ruefully recalls—into this one?) She shudders before the "fierce, ugly, armored things," looking away as the vacuum cleaner sucks them up: "I remember the sudden thrill of horror I had hearing one rattle up the wand. I was relieved that they were dead, of course, for I could never have killed one, and if they had been popped, alive, into the dust bag of the cleaner, I believe I would have had nightmares again as I did the time my husband fought the red ants in our kitchen" (p. 165). Final escape from the infestation of her mind is impossible; in her dreams, she joins the bugs "in the dreadful elastic tunnel of the suction tube" (p. 165) which her husband wields, confirming her psychological correspondence with the suppressed, not with the suppressor.

Her struggle against the insects is short-lived and unavailing because her buried self is not in it. Though she defends herself against infection with a handkerchief in front of her mouth, there is no denying them access: "At first I had to screw my eyes down, and as I consider it now, the whole change, the recent alteration in my life, was the consequence of finally coming near to something" (p. 167). She determines that the ugliness she had shunned had been an optical illusion caused by the distance she had maintained from the insects. Now, they merit glorification. Not even death robs them of their essential grace. Our narrator praises the durability of order that inheres in their exoskeletons (while our bones are worn secretly within, their structure surfacing only in the grave where the poor flesh anonymously decays). It is, quite simply, a glimpse of divinity that renders her own life small: "But this bug that I hold in my hand and know to be dead is beautiful, and there is a fierce joy in its composition that beggars every other, for its joy is the joy of stone, and it lives in its tomb like a lion" (p. 170).

Suddenly, inevitably, previous satisfactions are exposed as shallow. Like Henry Pimber in *Omensetter's Luck,* the woman falls under the spell of marvelous self-possession and quiet coherence; like Brackett Omensetter, the insects exhibit the joy of stone.[22] Just as Omensetter conferred magical weightlessness upon the stones he skipped across the water's surface, the insects themselves seem astonishingly light now that the burden of life has been lifted from them; stony, too, is their immortal arrangement, especially when contrasted with human perishability.

In the tradition set by her predecessors in Gass's fiction, the narrator tries to digest this stunning, new reality in the form of language. She encloses the insects in a series of admiring adjectives, and she reinforces her conception of them with elegant foreign phraseology describing their body parts and functions. She borrows the enchanting structural rigor of the natural sciences, then strives to improve upon it, reformulating it into an intensely personal artistic order; the advantage of the latter is what Gass terms "freedom from the *esthetically* senseless."[23] Thus occupied, she translates purely descriptive activity into creative activity.

The narrator begins to drift out of the normal circumstances of her daily life. Lying "shell-like in our bed, turned inside out, driving my mind away," she most closely approaches the ironically superior insect status; the insects "played caesar to my dreams" (p. 168). By no means has her husband ever possessed her so fully. Under his jurisdiction of the old, discredited order, everything was tamed, deemed disgusting, or just neglected. Innocence itself was a work of art under perpetual construction. Thanks to her metamorphosis, however, whereas she once had to force herself to look at the insects, she now has "a pair of dreadful eyes, and sometimes I fancy they start from my head" (p. 171). How can her family continue to recognize her, much less claim her? And how can such eyes ever again view their habitual setting with the old complacency?

Still, as suggested earlier, "The Order of Insects" does not conclude the exchange of one equilibrium, which is presided over by the busband, for another which is comparatively rewarding and privately administered. Instead, the story concludes with the woman caught between, uncertain yet yearning. The splintered reality of home and family continues to exert its influence strongly enough to make her doubt her revelation: "It is a squat black cockroach after all, such a bug as frightens housewives, and it's only come to chew on rented wool and find its death absurdly in the teeth of the renter's cat" (p. 171). Conventional duties and role restrictions reassert themselves: a woman does not have the right to indulge in these frivolities; her husband, certainly, would deem them nonsense. "How can I think of such ludicrous things—beauty and peace, the dark soul of the world—for I am the wife of the house, concerned for the rug, tidy and punctual, surrounded by blocks" (p. 171). Children and toys are formidable barriers that verify the woman's interior position. "Tidy and punctual" describes a brand of order which is in no way as remarkable or impressive as the order of insects, but at least for now, it remains intact. So our narrator has not resolved her situation in the telling. Increased perception does not guarantee increased potential, and we cannot predict with confidence whether or not she will be able to enter the provocative, "extra-suburban" realm completely, nor how that reconstituted self would appear. The very existence of her narrative does suggest, whatever her fate, that the temptations of the dark soul of the world have not been erased by logic, habit, or shame.

The title story of Gass's collection is recognized as one of the hallmarks of recent American fiction and has earned a deceptive reputation as a clinically precise depiction of Middle America. In the stark surface of the piece, which emphasizes the bleakness of the landscape and the paltriness of its pleasures, many readers have found a singular example of literary documentary which would appear to betray the author's debt to the literary realist program.

In fact, Gass is quick to complain of the regular misreading of his best-known work. To assume that "In the Heart of the Heart of the Country" copies a geographical location cheats the work out of its reality *in words*. It falsifies both plan and product:

The first thing I had to do was to get rid of any intention to be truthful about the place. That would have been exceedingly difficult and would have required all kinds of other operations. What you could say is, yes, something like certain of these things happened in a town like this but that was only part of what happened, not the whole thing, and I frequently get letters which say, 'You really captured how it was to live in this small town in Utah, in Indiana.' That just means they weren't seeing their town fully enough because it isn't the way it was. Again, they are doing something people frequently do, taking the complexities of experienced reality and bringing them down *not* to the complexities of the language which is, I hope, a rival, but to the complexities of something they then lift out of that language, simplify and then suppose that they have got a picture of their world. I find that dismaying.[24]

Regarding "In the Heart of the Heart of the Country" from the perspective we have employed toward his other fictions, according to which the dynamics of the lexical system rather than verisimilitude take precedence, we can recognize how representative of Gass's writing this story actually is. If the heart of the country is that familiar setting of the small midwestern town—the place, plot, characters, and style so often visited by the realists—the "heart of the heart" is an essence of consciousness, an inscape instead of a landscape, which derives from that setting and which is realized as the province of language.

The unnamed narrator of the story, a poet "in retirement from love,"[25] pits his language against the vast vacancy that surrounds and frustrates its generation. He justifies his insularity as staving off contamination by the desolation that his neighbors, who are uniformly decrepit, seem to have inherited from the town. "And I live *in*" (p. 179), he proclaims. He lurks inside his house in the same manner as the narrator of "Mrs. Mean"; also, he is ducking inside his own body, a self in hiding from self-awareness (while his cat brims to its skin with natural, uninhibited vitality and ease); and finally, to complete this nest of boxes, he skulks within the words themselves, atrophying like sperm in a jar in "my spew, the endless worm of words I've written, a hundred million emissions or more" until, like one of Beckett's spectral wretches, "there is nothing left of me but mouth" (p. 202).

In addition to defeat in love, a world of dim vistas also causes his retreat. Of course, we have seen that world elsewhere in Gass's writing. The Gilean of *Omensetter's Luck* is just as uninspiring, as are the photographs which trace a "Wisconsin Death Trip": "The loneliness trapped in these figures is overwhelming, and one thinks of the country, and how in the country, space counts for something, and how the individual is thrown upon his own resources, how he consequently comes to sense his essential self; and then you notice with a guilty twinge three generations posed in front of a small unpainted shack, and you realize that these families are as closely thrown together as potatoes in a sack; that, like men on a raft, space is what confines them; and that the tyranny of the group can here be claustrophobic crushing, total."[26]

So the poet shrinks into artifice to confirm his detachment from a world which is barren of love, energy, and potential. "In the Heart" opens by invoking Yeats's Byzantium, that poet's own dignified alternative to deterioration. But while the paradise Yeats contrives is a place of hammered gold, Gass's narrator has "sailed the seas and come . . . to B . . . a small town fastened to a field in Indiana" (p. 172). "B" is the diminished, unregenerate version of Byzantium, the eternal city of art. Furthermore, the poet's creation has come to embody the poet himself—an artistic project made spiritual project, in the sense of being the supreme projection of the artist's personality. As Frederick Busch explains, the poet is the town's spiritual complement; B is as inalienably fastened to his being as it is to the barren field, or as Yeats's famous heart is "fastened to a dying animal." Busch asks us to be guided by the pun on "to be" in the story's opening line, according to which the poet takes on the features of the world to which he has been exposed: "So I have sailed the seas and come to be a small town fastened to a field in Indiana."[27]

So our narrator has fallen headlong into his art and thereby succumbed to a terrible irony: the distance he has hoped to effect through narrative activity has not saved him from identification with his surroundings. Love's absence has hollowed out his handiwork, trapping him in the same fate that the other residents of the story—all of them relics, all wasting away—suffer daily. He interprets one of the inarticulate citizens as saying "that there were many wretched love-ill fools like me lying alongside the last bone of their former selves, as full of spirit and speech, nonetheless, as Mrs. Desmond, Uncle Halley and the Ferris wheel, Aunt Pet, Miss Jakes, Ramona or the megaphone; yet I reverse him finally, Billy, on no evidence but Braggadocio, and I declare that though my inner organs were devoured long ago, the worm which swallowed down my parts still throbs and glows like a crystal palace" (p. 201). Because he must, the narrator convinces himself that his potency survives the contagion of decrepitude; nevertheless, the steady accumulation of data spooks him. What difference is there between his own airless, obsessive existence and Uncle Halley's junk collection? And Billy Holsclaw, who wobbles in aimless distraction through the town's debris, is consistently recognized as the poet's exposed self. Trying to treat him as an object of contemplation, the poet discovers that Billy resists the advances of poetry. He is unbeautifiable. All the poet can muster under the sway of this Muse is a litany of grays: "For we're always out of luck here. That's just how it is—for instance in the winter. The sides of the buildings, the roofs, the limbs of the trees are gray. Streets, sidewalks, faces, feelings—they are gray. Speech is gray, and the grass where it shows. Every flank and front, each top is gray. Everything is gray: hair, eyes, window glass, the hawkers' bills and touters' posters, lips, teeth, poles and metal signs—they're gray, quite gray. Cars are gray. Boots, shoes, suits, hats, gloves are gray. Horses, sheep and cows, cats killed in the road, squirrels in the same way, sparrows, doves, and pigeons, all are gray, everything is gray, and everyone is out of luck who lives here" (p. 180).

Once again, however, we are counseled by the narrator not to mistake the Indiana that his predilections distort for the so-called "real world." He creates whatever suits his gray mood—"I must stop making up things. I must give myself to life" (p. 187), he resolves, feebly—and *that* Indiana is damnable, worse than any Gopher Prairie. To commit himself freely to life would be to capitulate to the town's poverty. Stripped of his lover's inspiring attentions— "Yet I was not a state with you, nor were we both together any Indiana" (p. 175), he broods—he cannot work on poetry, and he turns venomous. If the town seems hardly conducive to artistic enterprise, it can also be argued that, at least in part, it catches its disease from him: "Of course there is enough to stir our wonder anywhere; there's enough to love, anywhere, if one is strong enough, if one is diligent enough, if one is perceptive, patient, kind enough—whatever it takes; and surely it's better to live in the country, to live on a prairie by a drawing of rivers, in Iowa or Illinois or Indiana, say, than in any city, in any stinking fog of human beings, in any blooming orchard of machines. It ought to be" (pp. 192–93). Perhaps it ought to be easier to live apart from the swollen crowds of people, but the theory does not avail him. For one thing, "It's impossible to rhyme in this dust" (p. 191). Whereas the bucolic life and pastoral sweetness are debunked as "a lie of old poetry" (p. 194), so, too, is the romantic theme of a sensitive man keeping his chalice aloft among the philistines. Thus, the sterile poet condemns a world he cannot redeem; lyricism brought low, the poet trades the dream of Keats's "viewless wings of Poesy" for the desire "to rise so high . . . that when I shit I won't miss anybody" (p. 189). Impotently raging, he imagines the trees exploding, shaking off the joyless dust; the snow is like mass depression, "a pale gray pudding thinly spread on stiff toast, and if that seems a strange description, it's accurate all the same" (p. 192).

This is the hardest irony to bear: having retired to revitalize his waning powers of imagination, the poet is further stifled by retirement itself. With his beloved, so his nostalgic remembrances run, his words were buoyed by every caress; he could depend upon escaping along the slope of her body like a skiff on a river, and every interlude renewed his perceptivity: "You were so utterly provisional, subject to my change. I could inflate your bosom with a kiss, disperse your skin with gentleness, enter your vagina from within, and make my love emerge like a fresh sex" (p. 196). Now there is nothing to uplift him to where the sky only rarely "allows the heart up" (p. 173). He confronts a cold windowpane: devoid of interest, vision stunted. "We meet on this window, the world and I, inelegantly, swimmers of the glass" (p. 196). Poetry initiates no change because the poet's words barely consult the world; stuck in the window, they seem to turn in upon their fog-bound creator.

In the section entitled "Politics," our narrator notes the narrow-mindedness and short-sightedness of "the badly educated, who squander their passions on trivial matters, then senses that he has formed a treaty of sorts with them by hemming himself into his own idiosyncracies. Nostalgic longing is just as limiting, just as fanatical, a pastime similar to gabbing about the local sports scores. If the anonymous "they" are held back by mindless pursuits, the poet's eyes are "driven in" by a hypersensitive self-consciousness (p. 176). His inventory of the aged contains no one whose deafness and implacability is any more intense than his own. (What a contradiction of the title "Vital Data" is the desolation of hope that succeeds it!) In short, he has come to be defined by the closed space he occupies. He is as static and opaque as the house he occupies. It is not surprising that he thinks of transforming himself into a church, for that act would verify his psychological situation and would validate his vigorous self-worship, as his ego dominates the vicinity.

How far he has drifted, in the sorry tradition set by Jethro Furber, from natural ease. His cat is cousin to Kick's cat in Tott's overture to *Omensetter's Luck,* for it also benefits from unselfconscious ease. The cat shames its owner, who cannot seem to copy its lesson of how to live: "Mr. Tick, you do me honor. You not only lie in my lap, but you remain alive there, coiled like a fetus. Through your deep nap, I feel you hum. You are, and are not, a machine. You are alive, alive exactly, and it means nothing to you—much to me. You are a cat— you cannot understand—you are a cat so easily. Your nature is not something you must rise to" (p. 184). Calling his cat Mr. Tick is yet another of the poet's sophistries, for it remakes the animal into a clock; if its "electrical penis" is a rebuke against the ascetic poet, its rhythmically twitching tail is a metronome that reminds him that he is dying daily into greater identification with a dying community. "I am learning to restore myself, my house, my body, by paying court to

gardens, cats, and running water, and with neighbors keeping company" (p. 183), he rationalizes; but gardens mock his
emptiness, cats his incessant ramblings about the past, and
running water his inertia.

As for neighbors, they are withered premonitions of his
own demise. He blasts them for embodying the anxieties and
failures that brought him into their company:

For I am now in B, in Indiana: out of job and out of patience, out of
love and time and money, out of bread and out of body, in a temper,
Mrs. Desmond, out of tea. So shut your fist up, bitch, you bag of
death; go bang another door; go die, my dearie. Die, life-deaf old
lady. Spill your breath. Fall over like a frozen board. Gray hair
grows from the nose of your mind. You are a skull already—*memento
mori*—the foreskin retracts from your teeth. Will your plastic gums
last longer than your bones, and color their grinning? And is your
twot still hazel-hairy, or are you bald as a ditch? . . . bitch . . . . . .
bitch . . . . bitch. I wanted to be famous, but you bring me
age—my emptiness. Was it *that* which I thought would balloon me
above the rest? (pp. 188–89).

Despair determines his interests as well as his prejudices. He
cannot empathize with anyone but the old and lonely; youth,
once celebrated in his love affair, is currently represented by
the town's ugly scheming children.

Gass seems to be saying that one option for any artist is to
foster his sense of importance by sneering at mass access and
mass engagement, thereby reassuring himself that his gestures are reserved for the aesthetically-initiated elite. The extreme version of this logic takes the shape of an exclusively
narcissistic art, composed in shadows and tucked away in
drawers. (The strictest elitism is solitude). As it happens, the
rest of B accepts and reflects self-obsession. For example,
there is the ancient Mrs. Desmond, who, although she is

frightened by the scrape of flies against the screens and by the sound of "her own flesh failing," is hardly aware of the poet's presence: "Her talk's a fence—a shade drawn, a window fastened, door that's locked" (p. 184).

The structure of "In the Heart" imitates the fortress the poet has tried to erect for himself: a stylistic blockhouse. (Consolidating one's world so efficiently at least allows for *organized* solipsism.) Ronald Sukenick argues that the ascendancy of spatial over temporal reality on the page changes the fate of description in contemporary fiction and neatly applies to our narrator's method of "composing" himself in prose: "Since it is no longer the novelist's business to 'make us see' as it was in terms of imitation theories, description in fiction would seem to be pointless, but this is not the case. Description is too deeply embedded in the tradition of the novel ever to be lost, but its present significance is ironically antithetical to its former one. The contemporary novelist describes things with whose appearance we are already perfectly familiar (through photography, film, travel, or simply the modern quotidian) not to make us see those things but to test the language against them, to keep it alive to visual experience. The pleasure of description is the pleasure of a linguistic skill, not that of a genre painting."[28] The rigid appearances of these notecards is also consistent with Gass's analysis of a quality of human nature which the artist simply exteriorizes: "We are inveterate model makers, imposing on the pure data of sense a rigorously abstract system. The novelist makes a system for us too, although his is composed of a host of particulars, arranged to comply with esthetic conditions, and it both flatters and dismays us when we look at our own life through it because our life appears holy and beautiful always, even when tragic and ruthlessly fated."[29] Metaphor confers relevance upon all the strange particulars by coaxing them into familiar files. No matter how peculiar the river, to borrow Gass's image, man gropes for trouts, even if he has to recontrive them to fit his nets: "He arranges everything he hears, feels, sees, in decorous ranks like pallbearers beside him, and says he's 'informing' his visual field. He lives a lot like a pin in a map—he calls it 'growing up'—and there he indicates the drains. No, he does not copulate, he counts; he does not simply laugh or sneer or shout, he patiently explains. Regardless of the man or woman he mounts, throughout his wildest daydreams and even in the most persistent myths of his pornography, he will imagine in amounts."[30] For want of a woman, the poet takes pencil and paper to bed. By abstracting the world into catalogues, it is replaced with a language that treats everything and everybody like literary fodder; secured in the heart's heart of words, the poet indulges his "desire to gain by artifice a safety from the world—to find a way of thinking without the risks of feeling."[31]

To some extent, he achieves that privilege. When, at the end of the story, reality is epitomized by the metallic strains of "Joy to the World" emanating from a worn-out phonograph record, we do tend to prefer the triumph of withdrawal from reality; nevertheless, if the poet's convalescence is made possible within the house of language, it may also be unhealthily prolonged confinement, and any affirmation of the world, even one tempered by skepticism, might ultimately serve him better than do loneliness and inertia. Poetry loses its redemptive powers in direct ratio to its removal from community. The drowsy rhythms of the sentences that constitute the narrative "islands" concretely display the inability to resolve to move. As Tony Tanner points out, "The great empty space which surrounds the town is visible in the blank lacunae between the narrator's several entries."[32]

"In the Heart" explores a mental realm where content is never expendable; because the mind's life is the only source of energy detectable here, every detail is precious fuel. Gass assesses the value of fictions whose catch-all style—he calls it a "redounding of reference"—is the last-ditch effort of the artist to join into some sort of contract with the world at large: "Let nothing be lost. Waste not even waste. Thus collage is the blessed method: never cut where you can paste. No question it works. It works wonders, because in collage logical levels rise and fall like waves."[33] Parodically updating Henry James's advice to aspiring writers, which stemmed from confidence in the abundance that was available, our narrator hopes to draw meaning out of a blasted environment by personalizing it. He purges its foreignness to a degree by subordinating its inherent reality to the reality of his own devastated condition. Again, Ronald Sukenick supplies a useful corollary to the creative strategies of this narrator in his analysis of Wallace Stevens, in which he suggests how the sensitive personality can bear the rigors of contemporary American life: "When, through the imagination, the ego manages to reconcile reality with its own needs, the formerly inspired landscape is infused with the ego's emotion, and reality, since it now seems intensely relevant to the ego, suddenly seems more real."[34] Relevance to the self defines reality; the world is asked to make the principal accommodations. Clearly, the sections of "In the Heart" entitled "Business," "Politics," or some other public generality contain selective, personal impressions of details, rather than objective factsheets (although the accounting-ledger technique of presenting information tends to obscure subjective interference). Under one "Business" section, a tawdry carnival is described as a dinky, noisy waste; "Weather" compels a catalogue of lucklessness;

"Politics" includes declarations of outrage at the Russians for having shut up a dog in a satellite; "Education" digresses into an excoriation of the hapless Mrs. Desmond; "A Person" inevitably traces the perorations of Billy Holsclaw, the poet's second self cast adrift outside his house.

Billy's looming presence is especially provocative. Cast as "The First Person," and so, by extension, as the stand-in for the narrator's "I,"[35] Billy also represents the whole collection of "love-ill fools like me lying alongside the last home of their former selves"—he bears the standard of their desolation. That the poet is implicated by association is an awful thought to confront, so he reverses it into a more palatable one, conjuring up the image quoted earlier which speaks of the continuing vitality of his "glowing" inner organs inside the worm that swallowed them down (p. 201). Reclamation projects in the heart of the heart of the country concentrate on the internalized Indiana, but the charms of a vigorous worm are limited, no matter how fertile it may make the self it burrows through for the production of memories. As the poet himself admits, "When I've wormed through a fence to reach a meadow, do I ever feel the same about the field?" (p. 174) Means contaminate ends; the exasperating rules of refuge daily detract from the achievement of refuge.

And so, the poet clings unsteadily to his presumed vantage point like a vulture brooding over the dying, nourished by a dead love; meanwhile, "sparrows sit like fists" (p. 190) on the ubiquitous telephone wires which, though they may be "bars of connection" for others, fasten him to the spot. (His intercourse, communicative and sexual, is solely "by eye.") The childhood adventure of "Household Apples" lends evidence to the argument that life can flourish in the midst of decay, but it shows just as plainly that even flies "are so persistently alive" (p. 204), as is Mr. Tick, that the poet's existence pales in comparison. While the poet lives like an outlaw in the recesses of his house and body, and like Israbestis Tott in his wall, insects consume the sweet fruit. He confesses that his arms "had never been more alive" (p. 205) than when flies clustered about it like a humming sleeve as he picked the apples; however, he cannot finally afford the epiphany which tells him that his current aesthetic stronghold does not compare. "What have I missed?" he wonders, but only for a second before deeming those sensations false. Instead, he seals up his fiction: "Childhood is a lie of poetry" (p. 205).

In this way, "In the Heart of the Heart of the Country" completes Gass's volume by making unanimous the presentation of the artistic consolation as a double-edged alternative. Yes, art has the ability to rescue beauty and coherence from a world which will not sustain them, but rescue is expensive: immediacy and the intensity of direct experience are lost in the bargain. Only a soberly practical perspective keeps sanctuary from seeming like a prison, or transcendence from withering into trite unpoetic loneliness. There is always the danger that one's artwork may start to stink of artificiality, as do the "wood or plastic iron deer" that the narrator of "In the Heart" detests for their betrayal of nature. A closed cathedral, an endlessly repeating phonograph record that no one else hears, much less cares to hear—these images cast doubt upon the solipsistic creations which get trapped in the glass or on the mirrored page, until "all that lies within it's dead" (p. 195). The artist lies and suffers the consequences of counterfeit experience: life, which is tantalizing and dreadful, courses just beyond him, though it may as well be miles. And the pane's kiss is cold.

4

Willie Masters' Lonesome Wife:
The Flesh Made Word

WHEN REFLECTING ON THE FICTIONS discussed so far, we find that a disruptive paradox underlies the evasive maneuvers of each of Gass's artists. The fear that his "higher reality" may collapse or tarnish from exposure to the quotidian leads to the conviction that all worldly residue must be expunged from the polished surfaces of the fiction he erects. Wary of allegiances that admit the world, the artist survives by means of repudiation. The contention is that he cannot afford to be less fastidious in authoring his own being than he is in handling language, whose sureties he intends to emulate. But the frustrating effect is that the very materials necessary to the foundation of the artwork are discarded; in other words, abandoning the world in order to defend against its grubby incursions may so impoverish the artist that the values of refuge are entirely lost.

In his comprehensive study, *The Machine in the Garden: Technology and the Pastoral Ideal in America,* Leo Marx predicts this situation. He argues that it is a mistake to equate the desire to withdraw into a tranquil landscape which promises enduring value in an increasingly chaotic world, with unchecked escapism or a haphazard plunge into fantasy; it is the same mistake one would make in equating contemplative art with neurosis. For Marx, the pastoral ideal is more precisely identified with the qualities of reciprocity and equilibrium. The privileged state achieves a balance between extremes of collectivity, sociopolitical oppression, and technological "noise" on the one side, and the uninterrupted wilderness on the other.[1] Such is the nature of the transcendence which the pastoral implies.

Marx focuses his study on the nineteenth century and uses the terms "art" and "nature" to pinpoint the opposing forces which dominate that period of American literature. William Gass's contemporary fictions, however, require that we re-evaluate this terminology. Since Nature, in the sense that the term was relevant to previous centuries, has now been largely discredited, it is Art, the term that Marx burdens with connotations of the plasticity and deadness of the "made" world, which is now colored to provide whatever idealized realm may be entered. In the form of a language artifact, Art replaces Nature as, to borrow Robert Frost's description of "The Figure a Poem Makes," a "momentary stay against confusion."[2]

Of course, the contraction which Gass's characters invite by wishing to hide in their enclaves permanently and exclusively entails a further bit of redefinition, according to which the world—or at least, enough world to fill out their lives—can be stuffed into a nutshell. Frederick R. Karl considers this operation in the course of analyzing Gaston Bachelard's theory of "hut dreams": "The phenomenology of the imagination works to reshape the smallness of the space so that it becomes limitless, and it reshapes the limitless space so that it is subsumed under the small space. This opening out and closing down of space, this use of space as something which can be large even when small, and diminished even when vast, has its counterpart in the American novelist's use of spatial concepts. And it is . . . self-defeating."[3] A principal proof of the failure of this effort is the fact that, were we asked to create a model of the central issue governing Gass's fictions, we would probably find ourselves insisting upon various images of collision and stress: shelters frantically patched against harsh weather and barricades blocking siege. So much for idyllic retreats! The exchange of hostilities between worldly reality and fictional alternatives dominates our reading, splitting our attentions with their warring claims. The narrative consciousness is better described as a no-man's-land than as a garden paradise, and that sense is confirmed by the charmless appearance of the closets and holes Gass's characters generally keep to. And typically, the fiction is overmatched anyway: the outside world infiltrates its defenses, and barriers of abstraction crumble.

These preliminary points aside, we can appreciate the uniqueness of *Willie Masters' Lonesome Wife* among Gass's works for in this wildly extravagant fiction we witness a considerable readjustment in the power relationships that the earlier stories established. For once, the imagination is truly formidable, having sealed out and pushed back external reality with greater vigor and finality than any of the fictions encountered previously. The medium has reached its end, proclaims *Willie Masters' Lonesome Wife*. Language attains its rightful rank. It "began its life with the thing it represented, and became the thing it represented."[4] Telling precedent is found in Shakespeare, that glorious Willie, past-master of his medium, who also prompted language in this way. His virtuosity with words "not merely recalls the cold notion of the thing, it expresses and becomes part of its reality, so that the sight and sound, s u n, in Shakespeare, is warm and orange and greater than the page it lies on" (Olive). The world's reality is trumped by the disdain of mimetic duties, those grafts and ballasts which prevent the artwork from achieving a purified self-containment. Emerging instead is one of the chief examples in recent literature of how language can reconstitute a world according to its own spatial arrangement, because it "breaks off its old kinship with things and enters into that lonely sovereignty from which it will reappear in its separated state, only as literature."[5] From the start, we are thrust into a seamless artifice of linguistic and typographical display; alternative reality is now, and for the length of the novella, sole, uninterrupted reality. The conflict has been resolved prior to our entrance into the text, so that instead of watching the imagination strive to consolidate some tiny island of retreat, we fall directly into art.

These lessons come courtesy of Babs Masters, the title character. An amalgamation of narrator, story, and the physical book itself, she is the process of imagination realized and entire unto itself. She is self-proclaimed "imagination imagining itself imagine." Consistent with the theme that has guided our readings, Gass's purpose in *Willie Masters' Lonesome Wife* is not only—nor, as it turns out, primarily—to tell a story, but to interrogate the process of telling as well. Babs Masters is the imagination after it has been allowed the pleasures of narcissism. "Then I am as it is, reflecting on my own revolving, as though a record might take down its turning and in that self-responsive way comprise a song which sings its singing back upon its notes as purely as a mirror, and like a mirror endlessly unimages itself" (Blue). This passage meets its mirrored aspect on the facing page. *Willie Masters' Lonesome Wife* is a closed field, an infinite loop.

Fully enjoying the book's rewards, then, depends in part upon our willingness to relinquish the perspective granted us as readers of Gass's other fictions. For instance, whereas we contemplate Jethro Furber as he insulates himself with language against perilous surroundings—we are able to discriminate between both camps from our vantage point—we lose that conventional distance in *Willie Masters'*. Babs Masters' needs are blatant and insatiable; she demands our undivided attention, as a jealous lover keeps her partner on a short leash.

This understood, we are ready to investigate the rich, provocative metaphor that equates book with body. Babs, the lyrically minded babbler who monopolizes our attention, is a textual entity, a wordbody formed as cunningly, lovingly, and articulately as ourselves. She announces that her composition is actually superior to ours, and we are by comparison "unfortunate animals—made so differently, so disastrously —dying" (Olive). A figure of language will easily outlast one of flesh, and what's more, the verbal body is incorruptible. "These words are all I am. Believe me" (White), she chides, heading off the tendency to seek the world behind, rather than within, the words. To read her well, to attend her sympathetically, is to engage in a brand of literary intercourse that attains sexual intensity, for "how close, in the end, is a cunt to a concept—we enter both with joy" (White).

When language is handled by a master (could Willie Gass rise to such loftiness?), it has the suppleness of physical sensation. Once they are recognized as the real "events" in fiction, words contain the true erotic possibilities of the reading experience, "for to say Cecilia, even in secret, is to make love" (Olive). Gass lauds Gertrude Stein on several occasions for sharing in this belief in the potency of language. It does not merely signify an authentic reality beyond itself, but creates a reality in the very act of naming. That is the essential message of her reply to a question from a seminar student as to the meaning of "a rose is a rose is a rose":

Now listen. Can't you see that when the language was new—as it was with Chaucer and Homer—the poet could use the name of a thing and the thing was really there. He could say 'O moon', 'O sea', 'O love', and the moon and the sea and love were really there. And can't you see that after hundreds of years had gone by and thousands of poems had been written, he could call on those words and find that they were just wornout literary words. The excitingness of pure being had withdrawn from them; they were just rather stale literary words. Now the poet has to work in the excitingness of pure being; he has to get back that intensity into the language. We all know that it's hard to write poetry in a late age; and we know that you have to put some strangeness, as something unexpected, into the structure of the sentence in order to bring back vitality to the noun.[6]

But language is not revitalized by emphasizing its referential status. That has the opposite effect: it dwells on the belatedness of words, on their secondary significance. Surely the power of literature is not that of a collection of traffic signs. As Stein goes on to say, "Now you all have seen hundreds of poems about roses and you know in your bones that the rose is not there."[7] On the contrary, language is first and foremost about language, and words in literature are principally meant to communicate their own being. After all, is it Shakespeare's affections or his expressions which cause his sonnets to endure?

Babs tutelage—her instructions to naive lovers—also exemplifies many of Gass's precepts from his philosophical inquiry *On Being Blue*. "It is not the word made flesh we want in writing," he contends, "but the flesh made word."[8] Gass the polemicist explains that we are eager to move beyond the statement of feeling to embrace the feeling of statement. Obviously, this attitude would seem to some an open invitation to pornography. Gass the artist corrects that misapprehension in a surprising fashion. The problem with pornography is that it is equivocal in its employment of sexuality. Sex upsets the form of the fiction (as shown in the excerpts from the concocted *Passions of a Stableboy* given to us in *Willie Masters'*). Pornography counts on our prudishness to gain its effects, and they come at the expense of the whole design:

there is an almost immediate dishevelment, the proportion of events is lost; sentences like *After the battle of Waterloo, I tied my shoe,* appear; a sudden, absurd and and otherwise inexplicable magnification occurs, with the shattering of previous wholes into countless parts and endless steps; articles of underclothing crawl away like injured worms and things which were formerly perceived and named as nouns cook down into their adjectives. What a page before was a woman is suddenly a breast, and then a nipple, then a little ring of risen flesh, a pacifier, water bottle, rubber cushion. Without plan or purpose we slide from substance to sensation, fact to feeling, all *out* becomes *in*, and we hear only exclamations of suspicious satisfaction: the ums, the ohs, the ahs.[9]

Well-made love is not sloppy. Gass is interested in the pleasures of language lovingly applied. He admires the expert caress of the proper noun, the perfect verb:

such are the sentences we should like to love—the ones which love us and themselves as well—incestuous sentences—sentences which make an imaginary speaker speak the imagination loudly to the reading eye; that have a kind of orality transmogrified; not the tongue touching the genital tip, but the idea of the tongue, the thought of the tongue, word-wet to part-wet, public mouth to private, seed to speech, and speech . . . ah! after exclamations, groans, with order gone, disorder on the way, we subside through sentences like these, the risk of senselessness like this, to float like leaves on the restful surface of that world of words to come, and there, in peace, patiently to dream of the sensuous, imagined, and mindful Sublime.[10]

The pleading tone that opens Gass's invocation of the "mindful Sublime" suggests, however, that we are primarily unschooled lovers of the text. Babs proves to be something of a harlot, a body of language available to the inquisitive fingering and tonguing of anyone having the price of admission. There is no guarantee that her next reader will not be blundering instead of adept, dilettantish instead of attentive. (That the pages of *Willie Masters'* are frequently ringed by drinking glasses that have rested upon them gives further evidence of the insensitivity of past suitors.) Sadly, the majority of us are like the mundane shoe salesman, Phil Gelvin (a "gelding" lover?), with whom the universally accessible Babs is sexually involved throughout the major portion of the narrative.[11] Despite his presence, she remains otherwise engaged, her thoughts drifting into fantasy during intercourse. She would willingly surrender herself fully and undistractedly, but Phil, who through the act of perception "makes" her, in the sense of sexual conquest and in the sense of artistic formulation,[12] is unconscientious and, therefore, unsatisfying. In short, Willie Masters' wife is longing for careful use, for someone capable of truly possessing her. There are few masters of language, or, in the words of Barthelme's Snow White, another unfulfilled woman of words, preciously few princes among the many cluttered frogs: " 'Oh I wish there were some words in the world that were not the words I always hear!' "[11]

Gass's heroine does her best to restore luster to the spoiled words; her very existence depends upon it. She delivers a collection of referents for the male member, dubbing scrupulously, admiringly; she rhymes them for the sheer pleasure of luxuriant sound. Why cannot others follow her example? "If you had nice pleasant names for yourself all over," she reasons, "you might feel more at home, more among friends" (Blue). But while this Eve capers about, naming her habitat, her Adam persists in calling his penis a "thing-gummy"! The challenge of true love embarrasses his resources.

Coupled with the lover's personal failings is an obstacle to a satisfying union over which the lover has no control: the inherent deceptiveness of the physical object that lies before him. The ambiguity of the demanding text is further complicated by the fact that "a book is also *not here*: it is a platonic idea, separate from its physical manifestation and from its reader."[13] Even the most purposeful reader may falter after thrusting too long at shadows. In this sense, the yearning Babs (and the pun is enlightening) never really has her Phil; his condom may be redundant, for by definition he can never bestow his seed with assurance. The present text always conceals an absence, an awareness of a surrogate contact. "Empty I began," moans Babs, "and empty I remain" (White).

Yet another impasse is attitudinal. The artist—and by extension, his fiction—disdains the awkward forays of the same intruder he plans to attract. Gass himself has referred to the reader as "a meddler" because, like a child playing near expensive furniture, he tends to muck up whatever he approaches.[14] On the basis of Gelvin's performance, improvisation is better left to the proven creator. Predictably, not every reader will wholeheartedly consent to the textual fetishism of experimental fiction, preferring a less strenuous, less combative leisure activity. Whereas love relationships may be strengthened in the long run by shared travail, many are overwhelmed by it, and Babs will discover that she is trying to recruit a most selective clientele.

To compensate for the impotence which usually answers her needs, Babs must invigorate the creative/procreative act by dreaming up better circumstances. This is the manner in which she demonstrates the legacy of Gass's obsessive artificers. She churns out passages worthy of the most candid Victorian sex novels. She turns herself into Emma Bovary, her close cousin in the business of romantic aspiration. She stages a parody of Gogol's "The Nose," replacing that misplaced body part with the genitals of her dull lover. She waxes poetic, lingering over the words "catafalque," "lesbianic," and "managerial" as a spellbound lover might dwell on a tantalizing curve or rise of his partner's physique. She takes over the artist's obligation—this is truly the epitome of narcissistic art, as language writes itself—by sculpting concrete poetry:

THE EYE
BY WHICH I
SEE GOD IS THE
SAME AS THE EYE B
Y WHICH GOD SEES ME.
MY EYE AND GOD'S EYE A
RE ONE AND THE SAME
—ONE IN SEEING,
ONE IN KNOWING
AND ONE IN
LOVING.   (Olive)

Babs lifts the pen—that imagination-gorged phallus spent too soon—to assume two roles simultaneously; seducer and seduced, object and perceiver, she completes an onanistic circuit on her own while her lover dozes.

Through Babs's behavior, Gass wants us to realize that all art relies on the reader's willingness to enter into a sort of perverse contract. To begin with, the artist himself is a lover twice over. He "must woo his medium till she opens to him;

until the richness in her rises to the surface like a blush."[15]
After this initial investment, the reader is still to be lured,
and the author is after that specific reader who will accept art
on its own terms; he wants "a passive mind and, as in love,
an utterly receptive woman."[16] The ideal reader can be cap-
tivated by the beautiful and can recognize the rewards of immersion without struggle. (Admittedly, when confronted by
a metafictional work whose highlight is an intricate "strip-
tease" of language, most readers react like children stuck in
their strollers while their mothers stop to gossip—or for that
matter, like the gruff bourgeoisie at a gallery which features
Abstract Expressionist paintings.)

But not even ideal circumstances can produce more than
the illusion of contact. The artwork is an abstraction, self-
confessed. Like Pyramus is from Thisbe, we are walled off by
the very words which we find so titillating: "For example,
suppose there were imprinted here, as in letters of love a pair
of lips; could you, by kissing them, let the paper pander between us? Were I to stick my lips as thick with tinted gop as I
in fact spread hunks of bread with Scotch cream cheese, I
could not reach you—no—or leave a smear on any other portion of your world's anatomy" (Red). No matter how urgent-
ly put forward or lusciously laid bare, it is still the medium
which moves us. We succumb to prosthetic devices: "That
novel should be made of words, and merely words, is shocking, really. It's as though you had discovered that your wife
were made of rubber: the bliss of all those years, the fears
from sponge."[17] Art does have the permanence which its human audience lacks—Babs taunts us constantly with our
physical decay, as a vindictive professional might ridicule her
customer's feeble staying power—but it is the endurance of
the plastic over the corporal. With this in mind, we can for-

give Babs her frustration and cease to marvel at the way she hungrily seizes each opportunity for sensation.

Against these odds, a qualified conquest is made. There are simply too many savory prospects to pass up the bait, even if the bait is artificial. In *Willie Masters' Lonesome Wife*, Gass out-Shandy's Sterne in testing the possibilities of narrative play (or foreplay, in this instance). Puns, poems, and a wealth of linguistic pratfalls crowd the pages. The type swells and recedes according to the intensity of Babs's passions at that particular moment; by the same rule, the color and texture of the pages themselves varies, ranging from red excitement to olive reverie to stark white post-coital depression over the inauspicious performance of Phil Gelvin.[18]

Babs is heartened by having captured us through our "lewd" curiosity and makes the most of center stage. Footnotes, asides, and word balloons upset the normal linear reading routine, until a galaxy of asterisks rushes other concerns off the page. As in Nabokov's *Pale Fire*, contrary demands cause us to lose track of what is supposedly digressive and what is integral.[19] "But don't come crabbing to me about it—do you live in the modern world, or not?" (Olive) scolds Babs, sidestepping the likely complaints of impatient readers on the grounds that postrealist advances in recent literature provide ample precedent for her behavior. "I mean, the world is a nest of contrivance nowadays, isn't it?" (Olive) We are caught in *Willie Masters' Lonesome Wife* like Gelvin, though perhaps in not so intimate a grip, and we have little recourse but to allow Babs her "free and natural" idiosyncracies. Certainly, it would be outrageous to argue that an act of love should be rigidly enslaved by custom or measured by the clock. The novella is spatially, not temporally, governed,[20] and it exhibits a tendency to cling to the sign for its own sake, as exemplified by Babs's relish of the appearance of certain words and of the prettiness of the stars that mark her afterthoughts. Gass's writing enjoys itself. The book opens to reveal a photograph of a naked woman starting to swallow the first words on the page, in a strikingly literal-minded example of oral sex (and of the mouth meeting the tail, in the tradition set by that most famous of circular texts, *Finnegans Wake*). And if we do not appreciate the dizzying display, or if we find the whole experience of *Willie Masters' Lonesome Wife* too taxing, Babs snidely suggests we go to a movie (Olive).

Smudges, stains, and the interplay of type styles continuously unmask the book as a book, and, as a mirror over the bed might trigger self-consciousness, disturb the throes of reading. "The muddy circle you see just before you and below you represents the ring left on a leaf of the manuscript by my coffee cup. Represents, I say, because, as you must surely realize, this book is many removes from anything I've set pen, hand, or cup to" (Red). Caught up in the singlemindedness of Babs's pining for a dauntlessly poetic act of language, we have fallen into art. The framework of the narrative, in which a character, Babs Masters, is sexually engaged with another character, Phil Gelvin, dissolves in favor of increasingly straightforward analyses of language; Babs disperses into multiple identities and discussants, and the provisional setting of the novella opens explicitly into the "sweet country of the word" (Red). Demonstration gives way to commentary; with page meeting page and print caressing print, the book close-reads itself.[21] All contours suddenly expose themselves as deceptive; all orifices are really false leads. "You've been had from start to finish," the text derides us (Red); and later, holding us in a footnote's footnote: "Now that I've got you alone down here, you bastard, don't think I'm letting you get away easily, no sir, not you brother; anyway, how do you think you're going to get out, down here where it's dark and oily like an alley, meaningless as Plato's cave?" (Olive)

We "Return to Life" on command through the aperture on the closing page: is it a navel? a vagina? a drain? Alice's mirror doorway out of Wonderland? Now that we have had the chance to breathe life into literature, literature sends us back to life, asking only that we pull up the covers before taking leave of the book. Babs salutes our departure with a call to arms. Literary theory becomes political platform, as she prescribes a revitalization of worn-out faculties:

Then let us have a language worthy of our world, a democratic style where rich and well-born nouns can roister with some sluttish verb yet find themselves content and uncomplained of. We want a diction which contains the quaint, the rare, the technical, the obsolete, the old, the lent, the nonce, the local slang and argot of the street, in neighborly confinement. Our tone should suit our time:; uncommon quiet dashed with common thunder. It should be as young and quick and sweet and dangerous as we are. Experimental and expansive—venturesome enough to make the chemist envy and the physicist catch up—it will give new glasses to new eyes, and put those plots and patterns down we find our modern lot in. Metaphor must be its god now gods are metaphors. It should not be too cowardly of song, but show its substance, sing its tunes so honestly and loud that even eyes can hear them, and contrive to be a tongue that is its own intoxicant . . . . It's not the languid pissing prose we've got, we need; but poetry, the human muse, full up, erect and on the charge, impetuous and hot and loud and wild like Messalina going to the stews or those damn rockets streaming headlong into stars (White).

Words can earn the majesty of their worldly referents if the imagination releases their power, beauty, and dignity. Let the joys of sex inspire the lexicon and rescue it from drab utility. Love me, offers Lady Language, and how I would brood upon you!

5

The Tunnel: Recent Excavations

WILLIAM GASS has been at work on his massive novel, *The Tunnel*, for some fifteen years, during which time several portions have been published as short stories. While these "fragments" certainly hold up as individual works, they have a more profound collective effect, and although the novel remains essentially in-progress, the fugitive pieces can be roughly united into a composite picture which discloses the author's design for the completed work. What emerges, even from this somewhat fragmentary establishment of Gass's intentions, is less a departure from, than a natural development of the thematic concerns and the technical consequences that Gass introduces in *In the Heart of the Heart of the Country*.

The general outline of the narrative is as follows: A professor of history whose specialty is the Nazi regime, William Frederick Kohler, has recently completed his magnum opus, *Guilt and Innocence in Hitler's Germany*, a potentially controversial study by virtue of its relatively forgiving view of the Germans. Having come to the end of this intensely fact-logged, intricately structured argument, Kohler prepares to write his preface, only to find himself unaccountably blocked. Instead of the expected scholarly introduction comes a sudden out-pouring of verbal debris, ranging from the fanciful to the bilious, as though his subjective faculties, long-suppressed by the attentions he has devoted to his book, are now flooding his consciousness. These ruminations constitute the entirety of *The Tunnel*, save for the opening and closing pages of the novel, which are taken from Kohler's history book—a work which is otherwise overwhelmed by Kohler's personal history.

We learn, therefore, that like a tunnel, whose walls must be supported solidly enough to ensure that the project does not collapse and bury the excavator, the novel is an elaborate burrowing by the historian into his own past, which is scaffolded by the academic project. Compounding the intrigue is the fact that Kohler is actually digging away in the basement of his house, or is at least recording this imagined enterprise in such detail that its reality competes convincingly with that of the book on Hitler's Germany, about which we have little more than Kohler's word.

The title symbol returns us to Gass's predilection for inner sanctums whose walls are made of language instead of earth. Significantly, a tunnel implies a function of escaping to some desirable alternative, rather than just a stationary stronghold. In this sense, the passages of words are intended to be physical passageways: Kohler proposes to tunnel through language to divest himself of its preponderance, as well as through a presumably objective presentation of the past to a uniquely private one.[1] Of course, in the manner patented by Jethro Furber, Kohler is reluctant to expose his socially unacceptable activities to the public, so this is quite precisely understood as an underground affair; it is literally hidden between pages of his *Guilt and Innocence*, just as a pornographic magazine might be smuggled inside a textbook.

The anxious, fitful, surreptitious nature of the writing is central to our appreciation of the absolute status it comes to have in Kohler's consciousness. As if he were a prisoner trying to dig his way out of a camp—it is a concentration camp transplanted from his research, and a locus of concentration to which all his mental faculties are attuned—he must dispose of the residue he loosens in the course of his tunneling, which in the case of the verbal structure takes the form of facts, memories, mental doodles, and a whole world of established ground which Kohler simultaneously moves so he can insulate his movements. Gass is quite explicit regarding the three-fold difficulty the tunnel metaphor implies for the writer of a book built according to its physical specifications: "There has to be the emptiness that constitutes the tunnel, the void, the absence. Then there is the dirt that's taken out, of course, which must be hidden. Finally, there is the structure, which has to be supportive. So the book is three things. The debris, the negation—the hollow—and the hand that holds the hollow. So the book in a way has to have no structure, has to represent anti-structure. Only *my* structure, the supportive structure, has to be very intense to hold the mess it's presumably binding together."[2] The way out of the world is the way into consciousness; Kohler claws across, hoping to surface in a more hospitable environment, and down, plunging into the recesses of the self-interred. The reader is drawn into the ever-growing cavity as if into a vacuum, and we would do well to recall the fleshlike version of this activity in *Willie Masters' Lonesome Wife*, where a vaginal hollow served as the means of access to aesthetic joy.

"Such shelters from the world really widen the vision," justifies Kohler.[3] To be sure, the tunnel has had a variety of manifestations in Kohler's life prior to the one which he now expects to earn him his reputation. There was the maintenance tunnel which led into his old office, whose metal cover he was able to unscrew with a dime, and in whose labyrinthine darkness was rumored to be anything from a storehouse of final exam copies to a secret brothel. In fact, the image was also prominent in Kohler's childhood: makeshift trenches, tents made out of bed linens, the warm recesses of his parents' bedroom closet, and the natural cover of trees and hollows all afforded concealment from the world and the pleasure of being an unseen seer. Safe from the "eroding" awareness of the world, he could freely enjoy the "realm of the spirit":

I was, as I should say now, a true self-by-itself, and so a self-inside-itself like Kant's unknowable noumenal knower, when I crouched in the backside of my parents' bedroom ingle; yet I was every bit an untrammeled and fountainous will too—a pure gust of forthcoming, as Rilke might have written—a perception, a presence, a force. To enter yourself so completely that you're like a peeled-off glove; to become to the world invisible, entirely out of touch, no longer defined by the eyes of others, unanswering to anyone; to go away with such utterness behind a curtain or beneath a tented table, in the unfamiliar angles of an attic or the menace of a basement; to be swallowed by a chest or hamper as the whale-god swallowed Jonah, and then to find yourself alive, and even well, in the belly of your own being—in a barn loft, under the porch, anywhere out of the mob's middle distance like a Stuart Little, a Tom Thumb, or a Tinker Bell—unnoticed and therefore all the more noticing beneath the thick hooping skirts of a bush or the beard of a fir tree; to go so supremely away like this was to re-enter through another atmosphere, and to experience, perhaps for the first time, a wholly unpressured seeing; it was bliss ("Why Windows," pp. 293–94).

Kohler shows himself to have been something of a child prodigy among Gass's withdrawn artists, having discovered early how attractive is the privacy that enables one to invent with impunity, whether in the form of adolescent sex fantasies or heroic daydreams. There he enjoyed a rare advantage: "I was not an animal in anybody's little cage of vision, but they were surely caught in mine" ("Why Windows," p. 294). At once a source of potency and security, every secluded spot reestablishes the womb: "It is warm in the tunnel, and not as dusty as you might think, remote as an intestine in its fatty coat, safe from the haze of human shuffle" ("Why Windows," p. 299). After maturity, sex with his beloved Lou will serve the same function; Kohler repeatedly defines her body as a fragrant harbor, or glorifies her vagina as a soft sanctuary in which he might hide.

The peril inherent in the allure of the tunnel is one we have witnessed continually in Gass's fiction. Whether one digs or imagines his way into private artifice, he is liable to become enamored of the means and neglect the end; like the luxurious caress of Babs Masters, the peaceful confines of the tunnel may cause one to linger, then stagnate. (That was why Alice melted into her mirror without hesitation; Kohler decides: "The tunnel was more attractive than the rabbit was"— ("Why Windows," p. 298). It is a matter of refusing to face loose ends. Kohler's current wife, Martha, correctly diagnoses her husband's reluctance to finish: "What would you do then? You'd be a knitter without wool, hotel with an absent lobby . . . a horseless rider, Easterless bunny, Mellon without money."[4] The prospect of that dull, thudding return to life confronts the writer with contradictory desires: Kohler petitions the Muse—"whistles up a wind"—to help him "to end, to halt, to stop, to hush . . . to untick tock" ("Koh Whistles," p. 194); but he is just as likely to praise his work for letting him loiter inside it so long, "a stairway to a cellar" ("Koh Whistles," p. 200), he says, marveling at the provocative, secret depths of his books. To be sure, time and space cease to function inside Kohler's underworld, and seduced by that rarefied atmosphere, he digresses from the operation at hand. Thus, the tunnel resembles a cave, endlessly convoluted and full of tributaries, but from which the possibility of exiting-fades. As for the reader, he is at the mercy of the directions taken by the digger, whose personality hardly inspires allegiance. (It is clear that we are following a fascist, and an unstable one at that.) We run up against obstacles, dead ends, tight squeezes. Supporting walls, like our certainties, are continually giving way. "Nothing the narrator says is to be trusted precisely because everything he puts down is nonhistorical, everything is in a different world. The text is constantly cancelling itself. On the other hand, you can't leave the reader so mistrustful he has nowhere to go."[5] We have left the comforts of statistical data, the reassuring stuff of the history book, far behind.

"And now things have taken a strange turn," muses Kohler over the Great Work. Suddenly his motivations have lost their clarity and resilience: "I've dug patiently through documents, examined testimonies, also taken them, gathered facts and sifted evidence—data swept in endless drifts like snow clouds—seeking support for my theories, my beautiful opinions, in the diaries of all those destined to be gassed, burned, buried alive, cut apart, shot . . . the journals of those who mourned their possessions more than their murdered and violated wives, in the callous words of those for whom a piece of the fat pork they abhorred meant more than their children's deboned bodies."[6] Has he plundered the past only to find it deserted before he could offer its victims a permanent escape into the artifice of historical memory? At his most despondent, Kohler fancies himself a grave-robber, but even this judgment is undependable, given the dubious ability of language to recover the world. "So sentences circle me like a toy train," while seemingly endless lines of prose cage Kohler in; what had begun as a book written to the world transforms itself into a diary that confirms and excuses his solipsism, as "the long monument to my mind I repeatedly dreamed I had to have" ("Life in a Chair," p. 4).

Therefore, the historian creates what he perceives, and through his exertions to render the data of collective experience in a comprehensible form, he fictionalizes instead of objectifies. As "Mad Meg" Tabor, Kohler's mentor, described the nature of research to his apprentice, the historian is one who "cobbles" history, and his goals—proving unity, consistency, and the rigorous operation of cause and effect—leave his fingerprints all over the model he composes. Conveniently, "all fog is blown from circumstance, confusion is scared from the corn, an empty field is ringed with quotes like barbarous wire" ("Life in a Chair," p. 39). The historical artificer assumes transcendent authority. "If it were not for me the Roman Empire—here he made a hard white ball of his hands—would not, an instant—I heard his harsh laugh bubble from the crowd—stay together—and his hands flew apart with startling violence, fingers fanned" ("Life in a Chair," p. 8). It is the nature of the past to retreat from insistent probing. But if the dead are resuscitated, how can they help but reflect the image of their "savior"?

Thus, Kohler meets the absent world on the "windless page," which is as tentative a meeting as that effected by the narrator of "In the Heart of the Heart of the Country," whose window is the arena where he and the world meet "inelegantly, like swimmers of the glass." His subject is chaos, but Kohler, insulated by stacks of books on the office floor which seal out Time's rude impositions, lays down words like varnish. Meanwhile, anything that enters through his window is captured on the typewriter, neatly frozen and framed, and thereby altered "into art . . . or into history . . . which seems, in circumstances of my kind, the same" ("Why Windows," p. 286). No wonder Kohler is so offended by the record of *Kristallnacht*, that universal shattering of glass that symbolized the demolition of stable lifestyles by brutal reality. (Overwhelmed by the frenzy of that night, Kohler himself had thrown a brick, and only later grew to respect the fragility of windows, and to cling to the ceremony of innocence they symbolized.) In Kohler's extended treatment, Germany becomes "*my* Germany," while the excavation of Hitler's Germany gives way to Kohler's plumbing the German in himself that lies beneath generations of life in the United States.

Inevitably, Kohler discovers the same secret which his fictional counterparts share: words themselves have the capacity for conjuring self-contained worlds. It was the town preacher who first introduced a young Kohler to the power of language to manipulate, to subdue, and to confer potency. (It would eventually prove to be the initial point of identification between Kohler and Hitler for the latter was likewise inspired—by the film he had seen in Vienna about a political agitator entitled "Der Tunnel.") Following the precedent set by Jethro Furber, Kohler learns how a surrogate "tunnel" can be reified through language. Against a desolate background—the unremitting ugliness of Grand, Iowa, the town where he grew up—he invented a personal brand of detachment, "measuring a few great words read right against the accumulated weight of the wishy-washy, of tons of trivia and tedium, of Nothing itself—the melancholy experience of pure *duree*" ("Life in a Chair," p. 35). Language became a more reliable shield against the plague of desolation than any of the dark corners he had slipped into previously. Kohler's passion also imitated that of Israbestis Tott in *Omensetter's Luck* (and will later add to it the authority of scholarship). As did Tott with his "life in the wall," Kohler appropriated a landscape as unprepossessing as the carpet on the floor and, with spider-like efficiency and singleness of purpose, loaded it with story: "Whether I really hid behind my hangered clothing, in a hole felt the funny folds of girlies, or as pure spirit passed through walls, or sank like dust into the carpet and became its implacable climate and ferocious geography, scarcely mattered: I went away every time with the same result: that powerful out of the world feeling" ("Why Windows," p. 298).

Of course, using words to keep the world at a distance compromises their effectiveness in historical inquiry. Although the scholar accumulates more data about the Holocaust, he brings it no closer: "I populate my brain each day with further figures, larger numbers, longer lists," Kohler confesses, "yet the space between everything increases" ("Life in a Chair," p. 49). Research only formalizes his penchant for turning everything into abstraction, until it seems that words have lost their signifying function altogether; they collide uselessly against their referents, "like keys to replaced locks" ("Life in a Chair," p. 38). The whole activity deconstructs itself as doubt eats away at the supports of his project. As Wallace Stevens phrases it in "Connoisseur of Chaos," "The squirming facts exceed the squamous mind." Kohler tries to limit himself to the flattest, least embellished language possible—the language of sincerity—but every statistic triggers associations that fog the facts. He suffers a predictable chain of logic: How can these futile compilations hope to encompass the horrors they quantify? Does not all the dirt and clutter of the past which he shovels out of the way simply tumble back down on top of him, and do not the years reseal themselves as soon as they are pierced? Kohler pauses during the incessant shuffling of sheets long enough to doubt:

I have not, like my colleagues, overlooked the real arena, but haven't I given my results the neat and compact body of a book? Haven't I arranged my weeds like a court garden? Certainly I've not rescued God's Great Blueprint from a pile of soggy discards. I've not done that. I can't offer the reader Nature seen as a dump for divine signs. Only the foolish and the cruel can believe in God now. I haven't pasted up some poster showing a litho-nippled Providence grimly dicing us home as though we were counters on a board game—nothing so trivial or so grand. Yet . . . despite my care, my misgivings . . . I'm afraid that willy nilly I've contrived for history a book's sewn spine, a book's soft closure, its comfortable oblong handweight, when it ought to be heavier than Hercules could heft. History is relentless, but now it has a volume's uninsistent kind of time. And hasn't the guilt and innocence I speak of there become a simple succession of paper pages? ("Life in a Chair," p. 41)

To encode is to slice away whatever seems sloppy; to impose a thesis is to tie experience to a Procrustean bed. Aligning and docketing names and numbers as dutifully as any Nazi, perhaps Kohler is really motivated by fear of the blank page, or by the trivial pomposities of the aspiring pedagogue, and is merely exploiting a sensational subject for self-promotion.

I questioned people, gathered documents; I took statements. Cleverly, I collected incriminations, just as I do now, by appearing sympathetic, a little inclined in the same direction, with a bit of brown shirt bent or bias. Oh, I led them on from insinuation to denunciation, or I got them, in confidential moods, to go too far, as the case may have required, and show themselves for what they were, or worse, for what they wanted to become or liked to dream they'd been. They considered me one of the nurses of Nuremberg, later a lawyer, when all the while I was a hanging hizoner . . . an historian. And what is a teacher for if not to be accuser, counsel, courtroom, jury, yellow gutter journalist, frontier judge?[7]

If it was only posturing that kept the project together, then he is a fraud still, a pretender to the throne of Truth. ("Guilt and Innocence" are also the twin poles of conscience between which Kohler wavers.) Who is he fooling, prancing and preening like this before a callous mob of college students, or vaguely gesturing in the presumed direction of Posterity? Yet this is the direction that had been set for him by Magus Tabor, whose chair was his "only haven"[8] outside the dream of this sad world and in which Kohler himself now lives like the eternal eye of the storm. We may recall the haunting of Reverend Jethro Furber by the ghost of Reverend Pike in order to appreciate the subtle bond between master and pupil in *The Tunnel*. (There is also the example of Samuel Beckett's Murphy, who used a rocking chair to blast off into his own private mental orbit.)[9]

From his eccentric, fanatical, haranguing professor, Kohler absorbed several lessons: how to evaporate at will into the past, even at faculty parties; how to come to terms with history as a study of words, which are the most durable of human remains; and how to bargain with historical fact, when "fact" is defined as "permanent unlikelihood" and "counterfeit miracle" ("Mad Meg," p. 81). Through Tabor, Kohler was introduced to the Holocaust, and he learned how mass death confers magnitude and sublimity upon mundane lives by riveting them to permanent consciousness. What applied to ants, grasshoppers, dust particles, and cornstalks—the fixtures recalled from Kohler's childhood—applies to Jews— only in multitudes are they able to command our attention:

"Out there, in there, in the world—that life—one stalk, like one I had imagined standing by my mother's bed, counts for nothing, only in the mass is it fruitful, and the dust only in clouds containing trillions is it murderous and terrifying; ants, bees, baboons, live in families for similar reasons."[10] Words are stays against evanescence, as "language replaces life; history usurps the past, and we make sounds about sounds without limit; we steeple up a church to worship all the names we've given Time" ("Mad Meg," p. 92). Indeed, historians are not recorders but conquerors; they pillage and control as tyrannically as Hitler did in his imperialist advances across half the world. They "take in" whole races with their subjective designs, because it is human nature to require the sense of authority and the soothing process of cause and effect which historians provide. As Tabor lectures:

If the study of history is the study of language in one form or another, and if we really fabricate our past, not merely—weakly—live it; then we can begin to see how the world was Greek once, or was Roman, since every page of consciousness was written in these tongues then. All the central documents—laws, plays, poems, reports, abiding wisdoms, letters, scientific learning, news—were couched in Greek or Latin phrases, and the chief historians consulted them, composed their chronicles from the same speech. Don't you see that when a man writes the history of our country in another mother-language, he is bent on conquest. If he succeeds, he will have replaced your past, and all your methods of communication, your habits of thinking, feeling, and perceiving, your very way of being, with his own. His history will be yours, perforce. Perforce! I say make others—why be made ("Mad Meg," p. 95).

Alone in his office hideaway, Kohler rehearses the lessons of his master, which define history as a formalization of "the vanity of nations" ("Koh Whistles," p. 195). Accordingly, the German people can recapture some of their lost empire

by owning the words which remember it—that is, by imposing the German language upon history.[11]

To summarize, the historian proceeds from motives which
are ambiguous at best; his works are fictions—a euphemism
for fantasies or lies, however eager the public may be to accept them as something more. Thus, Kohler is apt to be measuring his distance from the Truth when he writes, or fash-
ioning a substitute for it, in order to validate his own
consciousness. The self abhors the vacuum that threatens to
replace it after death, so it finds a way to gouge its mark in
time. Certainly, the fanciful contributions of Culp, a col-
league who is writing a limerickel history of the world, parody and belittle Kohler's "serious" work. Culp's presence
disturbs Kohler with questions of culpability. Is Kohler trying to confront the past in order to relieve himself of a sense of
complicity? Has he succumbed to his own bloody mummery?
Yes, Kohler admits, "sour blood" is our common curse; it is
the proximity of Belson and Birkenau, not their obscurity,
which terrifies. "Or were men different under Stalin? Are
they otherwise in the soft towns and crossroads of our South?
in the dark crowds of the northern cities? Is there a redeeming place or nation? an ennobling institution? a kindly fire-
side, a humble hearth? oh, the world is full of good men,
good men with their good backs turned, who spend their
whole lives safely rubbered over while they remedy our
wounds, like the surgeon's hands stay sterile in his gloves."[12]
Frightening as it may be, in order to truly understand the reality of the Holocaust, we have to face the possibility that its
terrors were only the logical conclusions of some of the obvious tendencies of modern society—the ultimate embodiment
of twentieth-century bureaucracy. Even more distressing in
its personal implications for Kohler, we still must practice the
sort of calculating rationality, worship of organization and

talent for self-delusion that paved the way to nightmare.[13] Once Nazism is demystified and our automatic responses are checked, once the underlying commoness of the war criminals is exposed and the inhumanity of the concentration camps is understood as a human creation, their history infiltrates our heritage. Human expendability is clarified as a historical norm, instead of explained away as a devilish aberration in the otherwise constant flow of moral progress. The concept of the civilizing properties of culture seems a myth contrived in desperation; repressive regimes were not without their artists, and many managed to practice barbarities by day while reading the Great Books at night: Not only did the general dissemination of literary and cultural values prove no barrier to totalitarianism, "but in notable instances the high places of humanistic learning and art actually welcomed and aided the new terror. Barbarism prevailed on the very ground of Christian humanism, of Renaissance culture and classic rationalism. We know that some of the men who devised and administered Auschwitz had been taught to read Shakespeare or Goethe, and continued to do so."[14] Kohler is by no means exempt from this perversion of humane ideals. Gass describes one of his central problems in formulating the ruling consciousness of *The Tunnel* as wanting "to give grandeur to a shit."[15] Mad Meg's comparable insistence that "a book is a holy vessel—ah, indeed, yes—it will transmogrify a turd" ("Koh Whistles," p. 199) is also far more problematical than his confident tone would suggest—as history itself testifies.

Perhaps muteness would better reflect the message of all those corpses; maybe silence is the only defensible artistic statement to set before a mass grave. Loath to swallow the awful data of the Holocaust raw, we are equally incapable of stopping what George Steiner calls the recession of the world from "the communicative grasp of the word."[16] How can we possibly hope—do we hope?—to connect with the death camps? Would it not be more meaningful, after all, to decompose according to the pattern set by the dead?

Thus, history cobbles Kohler. Nazis invade his nostalgic remembrances of idyllic love; their documents trample his vision, which has become "as scooped out as a doorsill or a stair."[17] A field of wheat conjures a batallion of German soldiers at attention; a dream of the willowy songstress, Susu, is contaminated by the memory of her prostitution to a Nazi commandant, and the depravity that followed, as she sucked the severed thumbs of Jewish prisoners; even a summer of loving Lou is recognized as carefree and happy "because we had no history,"[18] until steeping himself in his research brings on the old melancholy brooding. Ironically, then, his tunnel betrays him, for it does not save him from having his "eyes driven in" like those of the empty inhabitants of "In the Heart of the Heart of the Country," whose unnamed home, like Grand, is diseased with dust and pointlessness. Kohler, a celebrant of death, a prisoner of a past he cannot entirely own or escape, is a walking plague; like Milton's Satan, he carries his Hell wherever he visits—wedding parties, sabbatical vacations, or even idle ruminations about the weather are contaminated. "When I write about the Third Reich, or now, when I write about myself, is it truth I want? What *do* I want? We drag our acts behind us like a string of monsters. I realize (I've come to it as I write) that my subject's far too serious for scholarship, for history, and I must find another form before I let what's captive in me out. Imagine: history not serious enough, causality too comical, chronology insufficiently precise" ("We Have Not Lived," p. 24). Tunneling furiously, Kohler is going nowhere. The imagination is daunted by the insufficiency of its resources. Worse, the cherished solaces usually supplied by the imagination have been disqualified: "I always find that my imagination moves me easily from prison to prison: study, office, class, bath, bedroom—swivel chair or toilet stool—there is an indiscernible difference; but when I would draw the snow back like a curtain and look out upon my island and my sand again, dreaming of sunshine like someone lonely waiting at a window, or when I would wear your hair so close to me it might indeed be mine, well, I ask the manuscript instead—nerves, nerves again, nerves nerves—and my thumb jumps—there's no passage, no exit from this chair" ("The Cost of Everything," unpaged).

So Kohler is seeking his own final solution to the problem of the Jews by vindicating scholastic activity. Until that has been accomplished, he will be "sentenced to sentences" ("Susu," p. 142), and like Beckett's Unnamable, equally powerless to express himself or to quell the need to express. His interminable discussions with sarcastic colleagues provide him with the excuse to convince himself of the importance of our consciousness in the midst of "this veritable hail-rattle" of events we shape and schematize and call history ("Susu," p. 138). However, Kohler's resolve is shaken by his peers. Planmantee, for example, discounts the particulars of human suffering as negligible bits in the vast maelstrom of Time, and he "brushed off mankind like a piece of lint."[19] He challenges the historian's faith in vestiges: "suppose events could be broken in pieces like bread; suppose, like when you break bread you reach a crumb you can no longer credit, as if you'd gone past the beaten wheat, the yeast, into the cell itself, then you'd have to back up, right? because you would have sharpened your pencil past its point—haven't I put it precisely?—you'd have to adjust your sense of divisibility until you got the right whole, right?" ("Old Folks," p. 36)

Herschel counters with the point that history is inevitably self-knowledge, while pretensions to objective analysis of the world merely deny the mind's true nature ("Old Folks," p. 44). Adding these to Culp's implicit ridicule of history as fodder for lewd rhymes, Kohler wavers, wondering if history is not, after all, just a dog nosing about the beach for the odd fish head ("Susu," p. 140).

The logical conclusion of these considerations is that history is "a process through which human consciousness perhaps endeavored to achieve self-contained existence" ("Old Folks," p. 49), which dispenses with the facade of the artist and the world debating one another like diplomats at a conference table. To accomplish this, and to test the operations of historical interpretation on a more manageable scale, Kohler dips into his private storehouse of memories and realizes that it contains ample precedent for the tragedies that affected entire populations in World War II.

If historical archaeology could in some small measure reverse the eradication of a race, perhaps digging into one's personal history can invest that practice with a feeling of a profound personal involvement. To be sure, Kohler has witnessed death and disease, sorrow and loss—enough to make him sympathetic, if not authoritative, toward those matters when their victims are strangers. His father seemed to take a lifetime dying; his mother, victimized by alcoholism, seemed forever a prisoner of nightmares which no one could do better than guess at. There was Uncle Balt, too, whose personality was an unassailable column of self-hood—an upright tunnel, with a fervid surface and a quiet eye, like one of the tornadoes that swept across Kohler's youth—and who stood as a model for Kohler's own isolation in adulthood. Yet the historian cannot consistently excuse his tendency to digress, and he often deprecates his consideration of family members as possible metaphors for "the nature of being" as "more archery into the infinite" ("Uncle Balt," p. 18). Perhaps he finds it necessary to repudiate the grip of their ordinariness, their numbing failures, as a means of practicing the sort of objective distance he wishes to bring to history. But it is part of "the fascism of the heart" to look to the personal and count it as a sufficient stand-in for something so unwieldy as the Holocaust. "I only want to understand myself, which is what I do when I interpose the poet like a napkin between you—that is, them—their lives—you, yes—and my mind's mouth" ("Uncle Balt," p. 28). Kohler confesses, although he cannot bring himself to recognize how that very confession discredits the validity of his professional research. To aspire to be a fog, or a perpetual absence (a "hole going nowhere" is the phrase he uses while mulling over the memory of Uncle Balt), is to cancel facts the moment they pass through you; certainly, the most disquieting feature of *The Tunnel* is that the reader may very well lose his footing as he makes his way through it and come to distrust everything—even Kohler's colleagues, even the welter of data—as mirages, for is not Kohler leading us into his own tortuous mind, one passage after another?

In this way, Kohler epitomizes the predilection of Gass's series of hyperpathic recluses in his metamorphosis of private fiction into public myth. Totalitarianism in politics is the extreme version of the willful imposition of such a myth upon unsuspecting, and far less calculating, victims; thus, we return to the machinations of Jethro Furber against Brackett Omensetter, which serve as Gass's prototype for failing to remember the fictive nature of one's constructions. Frank Kermode details the distinction between keeping aware of and forgetting the fictiveness of our constructions: "In this sense anti-Semitism is a degenerate fiction, a myth; and *Lear* is a fiction. Myth operates within the diagrams of ritual, which presupposes total and adequate explanations of things as they are and were; it is a sequence of radically unchangeable gestures. Fictions are for finding things out, and they change as the needs of sense-making change. Myths are the agents of stability, fictions the agents of change. Myths call for absolute, fictions for conditional assent."[20] This is the fascism which underlies the addition to fictionmaking. It is what is pernicious about the love of language when it obscures the purposes behind turning to language in the first place.

Consequently, *The Tunnel* explores the political dimension of Gass's consistent portrait of the artist as one whose dedication to the fictional realm threatens to become an addiction to abstraction, and whose preference for the orderly and often wondrous arena of language can make societal reality's claim upon him seem counterfeit by comparison. Yet the book is designed to capture and to indict the reader, forcing him to pit his conditioned patterns of reasoning against his emotional biases.[21] We are asked to judge without resisting implications; to "say yes to Kohler" as a convincing artistic creation is to credit the novel with completeness, openness—with being, in Gass's phrase, "all there."[22] So once again, we have run flush against a new reality—another fiction—which is all the more startling a confrontation when we realize just how unlikely a narrative this promised to be for meriting moral vindication and love on its own terms. *The Tunnel* is the sternest test to date of energy of execution, integrity of craft, and worship of the redeeming power of the word as proof of the value of that fiction which flaunts its "incestuous sentences," oblivious to that other world's endorsement.

6

The Aesthetic of Doubt in Recent Fiction

WHEN A NEW NOVEL ARRIVES on the literary scene, words like "avant-garde" and "experimental" are often used as descriptive terms and they occasion the same general uneasiness as off-color jokes at a society luncheon. Of course, technically innovative fiction has rarely been burdened by popular concern, much less popular success—tremors from Gass, Sukenick, Federman, and Hawkes tend to be restricted to academic centers, and the various crises of the novel that have emerged in scholarly journals are embarrassed by those which dominate the newspapers—but the moral content and effects of such fiction have recently surfaced as a subject of popular interest. The celebrated Gardner-Gass debates in the past few years, once relegated to college campuses, have since been conducted more prominently in the pages of the *New York Times*, while literary critics and connoisseurs have announced their enlistment in one camp or the other, often exhibiting virulence seldom encountered in this typically subdued company.[1] Newcomers to this battle ground may be struck by the paradox that whereas only the most naively optimistic would propose the reading of novels as a cure for the innumerable ills of contemporary society (however eloquently they may complain, artists only rarely serve as priests or legislators in the material world), many are convinced of the potential injuries that certain novels could cause. The parade of high schools prohibiting Salinger, Vonnegut, Brautigan, and other offenders of the delicate psyches of their students makes it seem that the evil novels do lives after them. Nevertheless, the question of art's noble purpose, and of whether or not America's newfangled fictionists abide by that purpose, remains fundamental to the question of how fiction can most profitably be written and read, and to what difference, if any, serious literature makes.

One invokes John Gardner and William Gass as opposing generals, not only because their longstanding gentlemen's disagreement has achieved some notoriety, but also because their respective manifestoes, Gardner's *On Moral Fiction* (1977) and Gass's *World Within the Word* (1978), conveniently polarize the issue. Very briefly, Gardner aligns himself with the tradition of Homer, Dante, Shakespeare, and Tolstoy, which delivers models of behavior, which defend against chaos by affirming the True and the Good; he opposes the swell of contemporary writers—he sends up the names of Gass, Sukenick, Doctorow, Purdy, Elkin, Barth, Barthelme, and Vonnegut like so many skeet to be blasted—who waste their energies in artsy obfuscation and faddish despair. Gardner is repelled by what he sees as "the elaboration of texture for its own sake,"[2] because it can only be trivial, however cleverly crafted. Whether it be due to willful apostasy or an unconscious straying from the right path, the advance guard has stumbled into an obsession with literary shape that neglects, in Gardner's phrase, "what is necessary to humanness."[3] "Either they pointlessly waste our time, saying and doing nothing, or they celebrate ugliness and futility, scoffing at good."[4]

As for William Gass, he is rather doubtful of Gardner's prescriptions. According to Gass, the only supportable demands upon a given work of fiction are internal; a novel is an elaborate verbal object—not a depiction of the outside world, but a world unto itself, whose structural laws must be derived from its own particular ambitions and processes. Whatever moral component fiction may contain is not dependent upon its presenting us with models of belief and action. ("Because fiction is a method which, by its very nature and demands, deforms, I am suspicious of it,"[5] Gass claims.) Instead, the moral work is the richly realized work. Fiction as successful linguistic accomplishment—that is the goodness an artist musters. Furthermore, if the fiction cannot first convince us of its internal coherency, it will never capture our faith in whatever ulterior message it may wish to transmit. In the words of John Updike, another author on Gardner's hit-list, "'Moral' is such a moot word. Surely, morality in fiction is accuracy and truth. The world has changed, and in a sense we are all heirs to despair. Better to face this and tell the truth, however dismal, than to do whatever life-enhancing thing he [Gardner] was proposing."[6]

Gardner wants to address the world; Gass seeks to plant a new object in it.[7] Against Gardner's doctrines, Gass places in evidence sentences, and not even Gardner refuses to name his adversary as the most proficient writer of sentences in America today. However, the assault upon the morality of literature which rather smugly announces its exclusive self-obsession is not sufficiently turned aside by Gass's good-natured parries. Is contemporary experimental fiction, by virtue of its unabashed indifference to the main concerns of social realism, less responsive to "what is necessary to humanness," and thus second-rate? If not, what is the nature of the new aspirations of such fiction to which we as readers must become accustomed in order to interpret the value its intricacies may hold?

Any reliable assessment of contemporary innovations in fiction must confront the common bias that equates literary realism and reality. Academic institutions further this bias by tending to define contemporary literature in terms of those writers who adhere to more conventional forms—Oates, Bellow, Percy, Malamud, Cheever—and to shun those whose efforts confuse the "continuity" of our literary heritage.[8] Despite its intimate relationship with the novel's growth of stature in the late nineteenth and early twentieth centuries, realism is a stylistic strategy, one among several; to be sure, the realistic tradition is contested by another tradition whose roots are just as impressive and solid. The first tradition, as established by Tolstoy, Dostoevsky, Zola, Eliot, and James, is intensely mimetic in its intent; it espouses theories of character, plot, description, motivation, causal sequence, and even scientific progress that imply an absolute vision of reality. The second, that of Cervantes and Sterne, which leads to Beckett, Borges, and today's postmodernists, proceeds from vastly different premises, premises which Gardner's culprits find so enticing.

To begin with, the novel seeks to become not a depiction of the world, but a self-contained, competing world, which is not so much about experience as it is part of experience. The novel transforms whatever it appropriates from the outside world—persons, buildings, words themselves—by virtue of imposing upon them a unique linguistic environment. Meanwhile, the visual arts, film and television in particular, render the mimetic function of fiction somewhat obsolete. Put another way, a new kind of imitation has evolved, one which is relevant to "fabulous and parabolic forms, or at least atmospheres, as modes which lend themselves . . . to a mimesis of subjective, internalized reality."[9] The "reality" found in contemporary experimental fiction is ambiguous and indeterminate, which may be viewed as a concession to its practitioners that their art forms accurately reflect the social world in which they operate. As Ronald Sukenick declares, "The form of the traditional novel"—by which he means the novel of social realism—"is a metaphor for a society that no longer exists."[10] This is part of the contention of the introductory chapter of this book: innovation is sanctioned by the inefficacy of the norm from which the innovative work departs. It is the integrity of the fiction which disowns anything more absolute than a provisional, arbitrary authority which disturbs the newly initiated reader. From this perspective, we can actually reverse the indictment against the anti-realist defense, saying that because literary realism functions by creating illusions of reality, the better a given novel imitates reality, the more counterfeit it becomes.[11] Techniques which confess their own artificiality—self-reflective narrative, associative leaps, aleatory forms, and so on—are comparatively anti-illusionist, and in that sense, more real than realism. "The distinction," concludes Austin Warren, "is not between reality and illusion, but between differing conceptions of reality, between differing modes of illusion."[12] Unsettling as this redefinition, as well as the debunking of a fixed reality, may be, it is only meretricious in unskilled hands. One suspects that writers of experimental fiction are no less desirous of finding stability, reliable codes of good and evil, and an inhabited heaven than John Gardner is, but they present their impressions, not their preferences. It is hardly an irresponsible role for the artist to undertake. It is fortunate that Sukenick tells us that experimentalism provides the writer with advantages that ease the burden of knowing that art discovers no clear road to salvation: "It has the virtue of generating unforeseen connections, and is particularly useful in a time when traditional causes no longer seem adequate to account for observed effects . . . . Causal narrative implies continuity and wholeness, but with the constant threat of discontinuity and fragmentation. Noncausal narrative implies discontinuity and fragmentation reaching toward continuity and wholeness, which seems more appropriate to a time when mystiques and their processes are laid bare."[13]

Criticism against formal disruptions in the novel can therefore be countered in two ways: first, the supreme authority to which an individual novel is subject is practical, in that it is specific to the needs and challenges—thematic, philosophic, or otherwise—of that work alone, rather than to some unalterable set of formal principles which may underly the genre; and second, innovation and expansion of formal possibilities contribute to the "novelty" of the novel—to the sheer joy of invention—which, as Bernard Bergonzi asserts, is integral to the novel's historical vitality and relevance. After all, he reasons, once the novel becomes "institutionalized" as a genre, saddled with the rigid rules and expectations which the term "genre" implies, it sacrifices in large measure its principal characteristic of "stylistic dynamism."[14] Indeed, the rash of articles that broke out in the seventies proclaiming the exhaustion, debilitation, or death of the novel were initiated by a sense of formal "used-upness," not by a suspicion that the legitimate form of the novel had suddenly been contaminated beyond cure. The concern has proved unwarranted,[15] but the fact that a capacity for freshness of expression was readily associated with the health of the novel is instructive for our purposes.

Intricate to the point of appearing conspiratorial, contemporary fiction reflects our suspicions about political "reality"; simultaneously playful and cynical, it includes within its own self-referential structure both the creative and the critical act; at once aware of its own potential expendability and of the possibility that nothing can liberate the individual so completely as an environment built of language, it carries on the one tradition which unites all opposing styles and theses: an overriding faith in imaginative energy. Richard Poirier makes this the guiding factor in his analysis of the contemporary American novel in which exalts "the performing self" as "the shaping presence" in those works which break from ordinary realism: "Life in literature is exhibited by the acts of performance that make it interesting, not by the acts of rendition that make it 'real.' "[16] What Sukenick calls "the progressive struggle of art to rescue the truth of our experience"[17] throughout literary history remains intact, except that now the task of decisively winning that struggle is more pronounced. The writers under attack for moral turpitude assert nothing so prodigious and unassailable as Truth, but instead work from an aesthetic of doubt that, remarkably, still sustains the compulsion toward artistic expression. Their novels do not foreshadow the perfectability of mankind, nor are their heads suited to the miter. Perhaps what is most powerfully represented in their novels is an abiding belief in the primacy of voice.

Consider the following passages. The first is from *War and Peace*; the second is from *Slaughterhouse-Five*. Both detail responses to the aftermath of wartime destruction.

"What's this? Am I falling? My legs are giving way," thought he, and fell on his back. He opened his eyes, hoping to see how the struggle of the Frenchmen with the gunners ended, whether the red-haired gunner had been killed or not and whether the cannon had been captured or saved. But he saw nothing. Above him there was now nothing but the sky—the lofty sky, not clear yet still immeasurably lofty, with gray clouds gliding slowly across it. "How quiet, peaceful, and solemn; not at all as I ran," thought Prince Andrew—"not as we ran, shouting and fighting, not at all as the gunner and the Frenchman with frightened and angry faces struggled for the mop: how differently do those clouds glide across that lofty infinite sky! How was it I did not see that lofty sky before? And how happy I am to have found it at last! Yes! All is vanity, all falsehood, except that infinite sky. There is nothing, nothing, but that. But even it does not exist, there is nothing but quiet and peace. Thank God!"[18]

There were hundreds of corpse mines operating by and by. They didn't smell bad at first, were wax museums. But then the bodies rotted and liquefied, and the stink was like roses and mustard gas.

So it goes.

The Maori Billy had worked with died of the dry heaves, after having been ordered to go down in that stink and work. He tore himself to pieces, throwing up and throwing up.

So it goes.

So a new technique was devised. Bodies weren't brought up anymore. They were cremated by soldiers with flamethrowers right where they were. The soldiers stood outside the shelters, simply sent the fire in.

Somewhere in there the poor old high school teacher, Edgar Derby, was caught with a teapot he had taken from the catacombs. He was arrested for plundering. He was tried and shot.

So it goes.

And somewhere in there was springtime. The corpse mines were closed down. The soldiers all left to fight the Russians. In the suburbs, the women and children dug rifle pits. Billy and the rest of his group were locked up in the stable in the suburbs. And then, one morning, they got up to discover that the door was unlocked. World War Two in Europe was over.

Billy and the rest wandered out onto the shady street. The trees were leafing out. There was nothing going on out there, no traffic of any kind. There was only one vehicle, an abandoned wagon drawn by two horses. The wagon was green and coffin-shaped.

Birds were talking.

One bird said to Billy Pilgrim, *"Poo-tee-weet?"*[19]

The affirmation of human worth in the midst of chaos is central to Tolstoy's art, which is founded on deeply religious premises. Tolstoy is something of a missionary whose matchless talent for realizing character and scene prevent his novels from descending into didacticism. (As Isaiah Berlin would say, he thinks like a hedgehog but composes like a fox.) Comparing Vonnegut's passage to the one from *War and Peace*, we find the contemporary language of Vonnegut to be unusually spare, hesitant, even disjointed; bewilderment and resignation, not affirmation, is the ruling mood. In his own way, Vonnegut remains faithful to Tolstoy's precept that art express "the religious perception of the age,"[20] which is from a twentieth-century point of view, a far cry from what it was a hundred years ago. Although one could argue that *Slaughterhouse-Five* pales in comparison to *War and Peace* in terms of artistic merit, the question at hand is whether it exemplifies less "moral seriousness" than its predecessor. I do not doubt for a moment that Vonnegut envies Tolstoy his confidence in his convictions; the point is, modern technological warfare is even more devastating and dehumanizing than its nineteenth-century equivalent, and its fictional products, Billy Pilgrim and Heller's Yossarian, represent the consequences of modern warfare better than Tolstoy's Pierre and Prince Andrew could. Similarly, Tolstoy's all-encompassing, ruminative style of narration—its ability to instruct and console— is not feasible in Vonnegut's novel. Broadly philosophical treatments of clashes between huge historical forces are luxuries Vonnegut and Heller can no longer employ; they cannot see beyond the senselessness and the fragmentation and the practical jokes played at the expense of the innocent, and incomprehension is basic to the kind of "hero" they present, as well as to the tone and structure of their respective narratives. Nevertheless, we are not exposed to any lack of concern in contemporary fiction; the inability to conclude a war novel with an "uplifting spiritual vision" in no way diminishes the moral impulses that gave birth to *Slaughterhouse-Five* and *Catch-22*.[21] On the contrary, it is the gap between the desire and the capacity for finding meaning—Camus's definition of the Absurd—which makes the so-called black humorist desperate in his attention to dire issues and unsure of the legitimacy of writing novels as a way of affecting them. Art can only manage so much repair against annihilation. Faced with such meager prospects, the artist's willingness to accept his failure, absorb it into his work, and continue to create is hardly negligible.

The next two passages have to do with characters in search of a calling. Once again I look to Tolstoy—Gardner would approve—as the standard-bearer of the realistic novel, and contrast a section of *War and Peace* with one from a contemporary treatment, Doctorow's *The Book of Daniel*. In the first, Pierre Bezúkhov, who emerges as the hero of Tolstoy's epic novel, turns to numerology in an effort to verify his role in the cataclysmic affairs of the world; in the second, Daniel Isaacson, son of fictional versions of Julius and Ethel Rosenberg, who were executed as spies during the Red Scare hysteria of the 1950s, searches his past for clues to the significance of their sacrifice and his own existence.

Writing the words *L'Empereur Napoleon* in numbers, it appears that the sum of them is 666, and that Napoleon was therefore the beast foretold in the Apocalypse. Moreover, by applying the same system to the words *quarante-deux* [forty-two], which was the term allowed to the beast that "spoke great things and blasphemies," the same number 666 was obtained; from which it followed that the limit fixed for Napoleon's power had come in the year 1812 when the French emperor was forty-two. This prophecy pleased Pierre very much and he often asked himself what would put an end to the power of the beast, that is, of Napoleon, and tried by the same system of using letters as numbers and adding them up, to find an answer to the question that engrossed him. He wrote the words *L'Empereur Alexandre, La nation russe* and added up their numbers, but the sums were either more or less than 666. Once when making such calculations he wrote down his own name in French, Comte Pierre Besouhoff, but the sum of the numbers did not come right. Then he changed the spelling, substituting a *z* for the *s* and adding *de* and the article *le*, still without obtaining the desired result. Then it occurred to him: if the answer to the question were contained in his name, his nationality would also be given in the answer. So he wrote *Le russe Besuhof* and adding up the numbers got 671. This was only five too much, and five was represented by *e*, the very letter elided from the article *le* before the word *Empereur*. By omitting the *e*, though incorrectly, Pierre got the answer he sought. *L'russe Besuhof* made 666. This discovery excited him. How, or by what means, he was connected with the great event foretold in the Apocalypse he did not know, but he did not doubt that connection for a moment. His love for Natasha, Antichrist, Napoleon, the invasion, the comet, 666, *L'Empereur Napoleon*, and *L'russe Besuhof*—all this had to mature and culminate to lift him out of that spellbound, petty sphere of Moscow habits in which he felt himself held captive, and lead him to a great achievement and great happiness.[22]

But this isn't the couple in the poster. That couple got away. Well funded, and supplied with false passports, they went either to New Zealand or Australia. Or Heaven. In any event, my mother and father, standing in for them, went to their deaths for crimes they did not commit. Or maybe they did commit them. Or maybe my mother and father got away with false passports for crimes they didn't commit. How do you spell comit? Of one thing we are sure. Everything is elusive. Revolutionary morality is elusive. God is elusive.

Human character. Quarters for the cigarette machine. You've got these two people in the poster, Daniel, now how you going to get them out? And you've got a grandma you mention once or twice, but we don't know anything about her. And some colored man in the basement—what is that all about? What has that got to do with anything?[23]

Each character is motivated by questions of public and private responsibility: how they can be made to interrelate, how personal and social history impinge upon one another, and how one justifies the actions he ultimately takes or avoids. And yet, there is no mistaking the extreme differences between the two attitudes. Whereas Tolstoy's Pierre is eager to commit himself to a course of action he "knows" to be correct, Doctorow's Daniel, bereft of that sort of manufactured conviction, cannot even spell the word. Whereas Pierre sees his role in the war against Napoleon as profound, Daniel sees his role in the McCarthy Era and in the Viet Nam War as utterly ambiguous. Duty, honor, allegiance—all crucial to Pierre's sense of self—have lost their currency for the befuddled Daniel. Again, unlike Tolstoy, Doctorow "suffers" from the absence of a religious imperative. Political and artistic requirements are not so straightforward, and they are often contradictory. (The artist needs seclusion in order to create, but can the political activist afford that luxury if he is to be effective?) The achievement of *The Book of Daniel* is not that it presents a definitive assessment of the American Fifties and Sixties, but that it promotes political, historical, social, and, yes, moral consciousness without falling prey to the temptation to dismiss any of these categories with oversimplifications. Daniel is a self-proclaimed "little criminal of perception" whose artistic identity is developed by his dedication to making "connections," whatever the cost may be to his personal welfare and composure. Plunging into the welter of uncertainties which constitute American political history, assembling data under fire—these are acts of high seriousness which appear that much more courageous when we remember that the contemporary writer is far less likely than Tolstoy to glean from them an earthly ideal of harmony and coherence.

Paradox and irony reign. What's more, language tarnishes our experience of the world, with each word, as Beckett has said, being but one more "stain upon the silence."[24] Philip Stevick is prepared to define "postrealist fiction" according to these unaccommodating conditions, under which epiphanic illumination of the sort enjoyed by Pierre is generally unavailable, and "the superior conspiracy of author and reader" is supplanted by an "eccentric new sense of the comic [which] has something to do with the authorial postures of the writers—innocent and naive, flip, facile, in a manner reminiscent of a stand-up comic . . . but tender and vulnerable, slow to figure things out."[25] In Vonnegut's "so it goes," we can recognize the helplessness behind the winking, the confusion behind the comedy. Whoever accuses Vonnegut of taking important problems lightly should be reminded of the platitudes his characters are forced to resort to—for example, "God damn it, you've got to be kind," in *God Bless You, Mr. Rosewater*, and the emphasis on the Sermon on the Mount in *Jailbird*—which are delivered in desperation by people who have nothing more substantial than outworn sentiments and clichés to cling to. One tends to envy that presumably less jaded audience of the past who may have been able to believe in such sentiments as viable alternatives.

Of course, the predicament of ineffectuality among recent writers is submitted by less sympathetic critics as evidence of a decline in artistic merit. Warner Berthoff is one who sees the wholesale withdrawal into deeply private forms of expression as contributing to "a literature without qualities." Because they call into question the very effort of making literature, Berthoff argues, our writers are intensifying the crisis of uncertainty by disrupting that final bastion of solidity and reliability, cultural heritage.[26] While we can appreciate his anxiety—discomfiture is both the theme and the desired effect of writers like Vonnegut, Pynchon, Elkin, and Purdy, who admit that narrative consciousness does not merely absorb the world but modifies it as well, and who make us shudder at the sound of our own laughter—we must also appreciate how well-suited this literature is to our age. Susan Sontag goes so far as to advocate that those art forms which accept the greatest amount of ambiguity are the most valid and that they thereby prove themselves appropriate both to the contingent nature of language (necessarily referential, sentenced to a state of mediacy) and to the ambiguities that constitute the human condition. Under these guidelines, the false dichotomy between moral and aesthetic pleasure and service is dissolved; "intelligent gratification of consciousness,"[27] a concept which denies that art is an ethical compromise, becomes the artist's primary goal. Instead of saddling us with moral dictates, great art paves the way to a moral response to the "extraliterary" world: "For it is sensibility that nourishes our capacity for moral choice, and prompts our readiness to act, assuming that we do choose, which is a prerequisite for calling an act moral, and are not just blindly and unreflectively obeying. Art performs this 'moral' task because the qualities which are intrinsic to the aesthetic experience (disinterestedness, contemplativeness, attentiveness, the awakening of the feelings) and to the aesthetic object (grace, intelligence, expressiveness, energy, sensuousness) are also fundamental constituents of a moral response to life."[28]

The artist's incorporation of ambiguity is partly responsible for the influx of new terminology designed to cope with a literature that seems to defy the old, familiar designations. Rubrics have been rushed in like so many safety nets to catch the windfall of recent fiction: postmodern, postcontemporary, postrealist, new fiction, surfiction, antifiction, metafiction—the firemen stumble over one another's good intentions, and still a good many novels are mishandled. More instructive than any one term is the fact that, collectively, they represent an awareness of an extension of previous boundaries which is worthy of special consideration; if recent fictional enterprises were only the death rattle of the genre or the perversion of a once-noble art form, there would not be all this excitement over what Raymond Federman calls, in *Take It or Leave It*, "playgiarism—imagination imagining it imagines."[29]

We are witnessing a radical interrogation of traditional institutions and conventional assurances in our society and, consequently, in the literature our society produces. It is sincere in both cases, and, for the most part, despite John Gardner's disgruntlement at the self-impressed improvisations and "tinniness" of his peers, it is not being conducted by barbarians. It is rather in the hands of writers who relinquish the orthodox myth of privileged insight. Their fictions incorporate the recognition that they are necessarily unsatisfying intrusions upon a dark and silent universe. The alternatives they pose as linguistic realms are not arbitrarily motivated, despite their frequent employment of aleatory techniques. If we are inhibited in our appreciation of these alternatives by an ingrained worship of verisimilitude as the measure of art's success, let us keep in mind that however expertly I paint a picture of my horse, the work that I complete has far more in common with other paintings than it does with other horses. To comment upon how faithfully I have captured my horse's musculature or glinting eye on canvas is to direct attention to my craft, which is to say, to my capacity for perpetrating illusion. By refusing to seduce its audience in this time-honored fashion, recent fictions must rely upon a different source of appeal and worth. Roland Barthes offers a useful distinction between the conventional appeal of traditional fiction, which is "linked to a comfortable practice of reading," and that of fiction which "unsettles the reader's historical, cultural, psychological assumptions, the consistency of his tastes, values, memories, brings to a crisis his relations with language," as the difference between texts of pleasure and texts of bliss.[30] The latter sort—the "uncomfortable" practice or reading, if you will—experiments not only with how texts are written, but also with the tools writing incorporates (words, syntax, typography, etc.) and with how we respond to the text laid before us. "What makes reality fascinating at times is the imaginary catastrophe which hides behind it," claims Raymond Federman. "The writer knows this and exploits it."[31] Nevertheless, the sacrifice of literary conventions which results when that imaginary catastrophe is portrayed on the page, when the artist's devices, shifts, fragmentations, and splicings are opened to the reader's inspection in the course of their reading, does not signal a rejection of the artist's mission (nor, in less exalted terms, does it mean he's given up the game). Just as the meticulous reproduction of a "slice of life" is no guarantee of artistic merit or social insight, the attempt to explore, with verbal acrobatics and typographical hodgepodge, life's arbitrariness and chaos is not by definition an arbitrary, chaotic effort. It may actually be as faithful a depiction of the imagination at work upon its world as my horse portrait will ever be.

"When writing about a boring situation, don't be boring." So goes the old saw, a standard of creative writing classes. Admittedly, the same logic should apply to the type of fiction under discussion: imitating a fragmented world does not license the production of confused or undisciplined art. What enables the best examples of innovative fiction to overcome this pitfall, and what distinguishes them from works whose surfaces are ruffled merely in the interest of stylistic fashionability, is the integrity of effort that comes from calculation and control. In *Living by Fiction*, Annie Dillard points out that the radical revision of art's traditional forms is not a legitimation of carelessness, because

the writer makes real artistic meaning of meaninglessness the usual way, the old way, by creating a self-relevant artistic whole. He produces a work whose parts cohere. He imposes a strict order upon chaos. And this is what most contemporary modernist fiction does. Art may imitate anything but disorder. The work of art may, like a magician's act, pretend to any degree of spontaneity, randomality, or whimsy, so long as the effect of the whole is calculated and unified. No subject matter whatever prohibits a positive and unified handling. After all, who would say of "The Waste Land" that it is meaningless, or of *Molloy*, or *Mrs. Bridge*? We see in these works, and in traditional black works like Greene's *Brighton Rock* and Lowry's *Under the Volcano*, the unity which characterizes all art. In this structural unity lies integrity, and it is integrity which separates art from nonart.[32]

Precision, attentiveness, and the power of demonstration, when rigorously practiced, become more than artistic precepts; they become moral attributes. Surrounded by threats of chaos or silence, both formidable obstructions to the composing imagination, our most innovative writers propose virtual systems capable of withstanding the disclosure of their own tentativeness. "Expressing a thorough investigation of the fundamental semiotic structures of our culture, contemporary innovative fiction illuminates in the play of meaning and non-meaning, language and silence, the creative aspects of our realm of being. The structure of our discourse is the structure of our desires and our illusions, our needs and our fictions. Recognizing that there are no privileged languages, self-reflective literature does not claim to establish actual meaning in the world, but offers an awareness of the meaning of our meanings."[33] If uncertainty brings our most accomplished authors down from the magical eminence of their realistic predecessors, it need not eliminate moral perseverance, to which the undiminished energies of contemporary fiction still testify.

7

An Interview with William Gass

WILLIAM GASS'S UPSTAIRS STUDY struck me as an extra-textual equivalent for the self-contained world of words which is so prominent a theme in his writing: books covered three walls and stood in waist-high stacks on the floor, prompting Gass, who was dressed to accommodate a typically stifling summer day in St. Louis, to apologize for his peculiar manner of "insulating" his home. As Gass spoke about his fiction, his speculative essays, and his thoughts regarding their inter-relationship, he seemed to be tapping into an ongoing process of self-scrutiny. The author is clearly his own most diligent critic. As he does in his writing, Gass shaped his answers with precision and care, befitting his belief that the word is a formidable event in its own right, and that "language is the vehicle of the upper self."

Both as an essayist and as a writer of fiction, William Gass has earned the reputation of being one of the most accomplished stylists of his generation. He is a principal advocate of the central importance in literature of the physical, even erotic, qualities of language—"the soul inside the sentence"—and

153

of the self-referential integrity of the literary text. A professor of philosophy at Washington University, Gass has consistently argued that language undergoes an ontological change when it is incorporated into literature, while the notion of a realistic imagination is an oxymoron that prevents us from appreciating the literary achievement for what it is: the creation of a verbal object that is not a description of reality but an addition to it. Gass has also won notoriety as a practitioner of and a spokesman for technical experimentation in recent American fiction, staunchly defending the aesthetic and moral value of innovative form.

Gass's criticism is represented by two influential collections, *Fiction and the Figures of Life* (1970) and *The World Within the Word* (1978), and by the extended philosophic inquiry, *On Being Blue* (1976), a highly poetic rumination on the nature of color, sexuality, and the reading process. His fiction includes a novel, *Omensetter's Luck* (1966), which may be read as an intricately-textured reassessment of many of the fundamental themes of American literature; a pioneering collection of stories, *In the Heart of the Heart of the Country* (1968); the relentlessly metafictional *Willie Masters' Lonesome Wife* (1971), a multi-generic, typographically-playful investigation of literary language itself; and several sections of a mammoth work-in-progress, *The Tunnel*, which have appeared in a variety of periodicals over the past fifteen years.

Arthur M. Saltzman

Q. In 1981 you did an interview with Jan Garden Castro in which you said that beauty and morality are aspects of form rather than of belief, and what matters is that what you say is well said, not whether it is attractive or true. I am wondering where a writer's beliefs *do* belong in his art. Is having a point to make about the world a valid reason for writing fiction? Certainly there are many novelists who hope to teach us something about the world. Is that desire applicable to the way literature affects us?

A. Certainly that's a motive for writing, but I don't think it's enough to justify it. There are lots of personal reasons why one writes, and they may include a message or attitude or self-expression—there are millions of possibilities, but these exist for people who are not writing, too. Now the question is whether or not you can succeed in forming your opinions or attitudes in such a way that they are artistically interesting. When that's done, they become artistically viable even if people don't share them and are not persuaded. In fact, the more you tend to make your opinions artistically interesting, the less rhetorical effectiveness they tend to have. They tend to get distanced and to become objects of contemplation, not belief.

Q. One of the problems I have in coming to terms with the primacy of the word over the conviction is knowing what to do with artists who are generally accepted as important, even great, but who perhaps are not so stylistically elegant. Dreiser, for example.

A. I don't think Dreiser is worth bothering with, except as a social phenomenon. He's certainly historically important, and expressive of ideas and attitudes and interests, but he can't write. Again, there are two elements here. There is the notion of a construction that you might talk about somewhat independently of the particular words used to form a story like *An American Tragedy*. But for my money, work like that, as opposed, say, to Trollope or someone else whose writing, while it may not be line-by-line distinguished, is nuanced and careful and has constructions of interest . . . I don't find much of that in someone like Dreiser.

Q. I'm going to paraphrase you now. An author's responsibility is to the coherence of his system. As this theory applies to *Omensetter's Luck*, what is it that leads to Furber's breakdown in that novel? Is it that his system is somehow fractured by contact with Omensetter, or are there imperfections inherent in the system which confrontation with Omensetter merely emphasizes or brings to light?

A. Oh, yes, the latter, certainly. And of course, Furber is confronted by the fact that his own system of ideas might really be true. I mean, it was okay to believe it as long as it really *wasn't so*. That's true for a lot of people. Beliefs are held in a very strange way. We notice the contradictions in people's behaviors—they believe this and they do that, so that you can measure differences. For instance, I believe that fire burns, and so I don't put my hand in it. I believe that there is a God, but then I do all kinds of things which suggest that my belief, even though it's deeply held, is a different kind of thing. I think that if something happened to make people believe that there was a God, *really*, then the confrontation with the consequences of that would be terrifying. I mean, if there really were a Being controlling the world, look what this Being is doing! What happens to Furber is that his rhetoric is brought home. It was tolerable as long as it was held in rhetorical abeyance, but as soon as it becomes more than that, it becomes intolerable.

Q. What happens when you have a character who has the capacity for imposing his rhetorical constructions on the world?

A. That is, of course, what everybody does, it seems to me. Furber is just very good at it. He's aware of it, and he tries to slip by problems by creating more rhetoric. And there's a point at which he's unable to do that . . . because he's confronted by somebody who apparently has no rhetoric at all.

Q. You've mentioned elsewhere that Furber was your hero, or at least your main character, because he's the one with the language. The hero is the one with the good lines. Is that the case with all literature?

A. Yes. In this inverted way, Furber is the hero, though not in any ordinary sense. He is certainly the central, pivotal character because he has the best lines, and people have been puzzled about that because it moves him toward a heroic status. I was just reading a book on the origins of eloquence—it was talking about the Elizabethan period—and the point being made in that book is that a great many of the dramatic moments in Shakespeare, for example, succeed mainly because the rhetoric succeeds. Psychological shifts, changes of heart, all sorts of things happen which are inexplicable, except that if the speech is good enough, it works. The same thing is true in the way I go at things.

Q. What is it that finally separates Gass the artist from Furber the artist, or from the other obsessive, rhetorically minded characters in your work?

A. The differentiation has to do with whether or not an author can take characters with varying points of view and lend them appropriate language. If he couldn't, then one would have to ask if this is a character or if this is the author, because the author hasn't given a language to a character, but just tacked a character's name on his own language. That's a problem I have in the novel I'm working on presently.

There's only one character. All the language belongs to that character. And yet, certain characters have to emerge, with language intact, with that system. That's simply an explicit statement of what's a hidden problem when the author is not present but is creating characters. Here the narrator is present and is creating characters.

Q. Even though they are attractive by virtue of their language, many of your most effective characters are not attractive personally.

A. No, the narrator of the new novel is not.

Q. You've spoken of Satan before, and of Iago, and of the fascination of evil. You are drawn to it in your own writing as well. Does that suggest a pessimistic view of the world, or is it rather that Nazism in *The Tunnel* is interesting as a formal challenge, as an organizational structure?

A. Both of those things are the case. I actually was working this morning on just that idea. The superior importance of evil, in the sense that that's what we really believe in. The rhetorical stance I was taking, or giving to the character, was that there are no heroes we can really believe in anymore, but we *do* believe in our villains.

Q. They are more substantial, somehow.

A. Yes, and more knowledge will not take our dislike of Attila the Hun or Hitler away. In fact, what is going to be bad about my narrator's problem is that I have probably written a book in which he sees some good in Hitler, which is inexcusable. To see some bad in Albert Schweitzer is usual. What I have the narrator start talking about is evil's greater stature in our reality. As a writer, I've over-extended the case. I'm giving it to Kohler—he is thinking this, uttering the cynicisms of an extreme character—but I hope *I* know what the weaknesses of those arguments are, and can back off and undercut them if I need to. But I've got to make that seem convincing for the reader at the time. Otherwise, the character doesn't seem to be feeling these things.

Q. Is *The Tunnel* near completion?

A. It's coming along pretty well now. I know what its structure is, how long it's going to be. Most of the things are laid out. It's a matter of finally executing them, a matter of staying in the book continuously for maybe another year.

Q. You've spoken of "character" several times, and I wonder if terms such as "character" and "plot" retain their relevance in your literary theory. What happens to them once we see a novel as a self-contained referential system? Do such traditional means of evaluating fiction still hold up?

A. They get redefined. I don't think they drop out at all. There are levels of structure in which those things are very important. For me, a character is really a voice and a source of language. If one has really created a character, then he knows that that character is going to have its language and will be speaking in a certain way. Words are going to come out from that source either as direct speech or as a means of dictating the language you use in the third person to describe scenes or that individual from outside. It starts giving you the words, the gestures, everything. It's a source of language. Although I don't write like Stanley Elkin at all, I think that what Stanley does is something a lot of us do, and that is find a voice. But I think what Stanley does is find an occupation and then lets the occupation speak. That occupation creates a voice, which then creates a character, and gives him his book.

Q. And yet for many writers, including Elkin and yourself, all the characters seem to have this propensity for highly lyrical language. I think of Henry James's housekeepers, too. It's as if this kind of writer wants to do justice to his situation by giving every character a vocabulary. Does that compromise the effect of his novel?

A. No, that's just anti-realism. In the first story I wrote, I tried to cut the vocabulary down because I had a character of a limited vocabulary. But I still wanted poetry. Now I don't try to do that. Faulkner doesn't do that. Shakespeare doesn't do it. Dickens doesn't do it. It is perfectly legitimate to make that restriction as a formal problem. You could do it if you wanted to. But it doesn't seem in any way necessary. You can choose to release your language for all your characters, or you can decide to restrict it in certain ways. Both are perfectly reasonable decisions of a thoroughly technical sort. To say a plumber must speak in a certain way is part of a tradition that you can accept. But it's only a convention.

Q. In a recent essay of yours, "Representation and the War for Reality," you argue in part that human consciousness cannot apprehend reality without the interference of language. All mental acts are dependent upon being constructed in words before we are able to make use of them. Depending on one's point of view, language is either a barrier or a shield. It's a matter of attitude how we deal with this inevitability. I am curious to know if the beauty of the verbal world is for you adequate compensation for not being able to get at the physical world more directly.

A. No, I think it's not adequate. Art is not the solution to everything. In fact, it solves hardly anything. It may make life bearable. One of the things that's involved in the idea of *The*

Tunnel is the attempt to get outside language. The fact is that language creates a world which does protect us and which we can live in, but it also bamboozles us. This is also true of emotions. Love is wonderful while you're in it, but it is also illusory, and the same thing happens with language. It is certainly not adequate. I would certainly not want to suggest that because there are beautiful things all the moral problems go away. They don't at all.

Q. You've called literary realism a contradiction in terms. Solidity of specification, the appearance of factual reality in works of literature—are these results of mistaken impressions about what art truly is?

A. The only real difference between literary realism, which is a perfectly legitimate mode, and formal alternatives which reject it, is that literary realists make the mistake of thinking that the world is like that, and that this justifies the constructions they make. That is a mistake. Now the real artists among the Great Realists didn't allow that to happen. Even now you have people like Robbe-Grillet, who is a realist—he just has a different conception of reality. He creates a world which is nothing like Dickens's, but both might think, "Ah, but this is the way it really *is*." But we will read either if they are good enough writers, not because they may happen to create a world which moves us to say it's "the real thing."

Q. Ronald Sukenick said something to the effect that every generation's best writers see themselves as moving closer to their conception of realism, so that realism is actually a very fluid, subjective notion, even as a convention for literature. He also talks about setting himself formal tasks. He will have a guiding rhythm or metaphor for a story—an arbitrary beginning to generate language. Do you ever begin in this fashion?

A. If it's a single short story, that choice may dominate all the way through; if it's a novel, there will be several of those choices, right down to the shaping of paragraphs. Often it's not an arbitrary choice. You start to work with a particular passage, and it hasn't got any shape. So you foist a possibility on it, and then force it. So it's an exchange. Often the passage suggests its shape, but it's not all there—you have to push. I do that constantly—page after page almost. That's one reason why I'm interested in rhetorical tropes and schemes. They're really the syntax of paragraphs and longer formulas. They are ordering processes, and I couldn't get on without those things. I have an interesting exchange at times with my wife, who's an architect. When she has a new problem, like the site plan for a school which she's working on now, she tends to approach the problem with all sorts of considerations, while I would come at the problem, as do many of the architects I admire, with all kinds of geometrical potentialities sitting there quite abstractly, quite independently of the problem, and the problem then gets molded. It has to squeeze itself into the abstractions, and not the other way around.

Q. According to the terminology of "Representation and the War for Reality," does that make you a "thin" rather than a "thick"?

A. From that direction, I would be a thin, yes.

Q. It struck me how in that article you seemed to be claiming a very definite distinction between those who favor design and those who admit data in a comparatively unqualified way. It seems that both are natural aspects of the human mind.

A. Oh, sure, You're moving to the center position. You've got a model, but it's a matter of which end you move from, and I tend to move from the abstract end. Mary tends to move from the other. You can always tell where one arrives from.

Q. I'm also reminded of your essay "Carrots, Noses, Snow, Rose, Roses," which says that words undergo an ontological transformation when placed in a snowman's face. I'm inclined to say, "Look at that snowman's nose. Now there's a clever use of a carrot," which doesn't let go of either end of the carrot's reality.

A. Again, both parts of it are natural. Both are real. It's a matter of the reader's willingness to entertain that additional real claim.

Q. You've argued that the artist's ultimate effect on society is a revolution of consciousness. This appears to be the burden of your essay "The Artist and Society." Is this a more qualified effect than what the social realist hopes to achieve?

A. Mine is a more radical stance. Just from the socio-political side of it, somebody tends to be regarded as a realist if he is working in a mode that people around him recognize as Reality. If he is trying to change things, he's changing them within that system of perceiving things. He's accepting that system, buying it. He has the possibility of making some changes within the basic framework. But if he really changes the way the world is apprehended . . . that's a much more radical move.

Q. This is one of the perplexities of the self-referential language system, it seems to me. It sounds as though any connections it may have with external, socio-political reality calls into question the artwork's integrity, its self-sufficiency. Does the concept of a self-contained system limit the potential for confronting the world?

A. No, I think we do it all the time. It's a question of how wisely we do it, how skeptically we do it, how playfully we do it. We can take the rearrangement of consciousness that you get in Beckett and then suddenly see things in the world. Now that isn't what makes Beckett a great artist, but it's a consequence of great art. The world suddenly is what Beckett says it is in the play, and when you leave that play, the world is still a little bit what it is in the play. So what you've created is another model, a rich and wonderful model, and it does the job.

Q. You've said that what keeps his characters alive is the flow of language, and his characters often become so obsessed with language that it replaces the world. I think of Krapp luxuriating in the word "spool"—it's far more real to him than the spool that sits in front of him on the table. That's potentially dangerous.

A. Sure. Very. It's one of the topics of *The Tunnel*. It's a constant tension in art. That's why I have this historian. It is a very tempting doctrine to suppose that history is basically linguistic. That means that as soon as you remove that ultimate ground, you have simply power plays. This is the reason why, although I'm very interested in alternative theory construction in philosophy, I would hold that there is in fact a reality which grounds our doctrines, and by which we can correct them. It's not just a kind of relativism between systems. I think that holds true for art, because artistic systems are not trying to make those statements. James was worried about this, although in the moral sphere. When you mistake artistic values for ethical ones . . .

Q. Something like anti-Semitism can be awfully coherent.

A. Indeed. And therefore immediately attractive.

Q. It makes you as an artist very influential. It gives you political responsibility.

A. Well, you have the same political responsibility that any citizen does to keep from believing stupidities. To the degree that you want to prompt political ideas in your work—as I say, the motives for writing are manifold, and it is not impossible to write beautifully *and* have a point of view—it seems very likely that you have to have responsible ones. That's why, for instance, I've never been very fond of Sartre, not only theoretically but personally, because I take him to be frivolous. With all that stuff about commitment, you look at his life—he really didn't do it. He had power and influence and used it frivolously. He adopted points of view which were dramatic and went from one silliness to another, what with having to support Stalin and then Mao . . . and that's irresponsible. A lot of the French intellectual tradition from Pascal on is infected with a kind of gamesmanship which I associate with *art*. I think it is one of the things Valéry saw very well, very clearly, and was one of the reasons why he hated Pascal. You even see that point of view being carried on in criticism: adopting for certain areas a kind of play which involves rhetorical drama. I suppose as long as you do it in criticism it really doesn't matter; you say dumb things about Flaubert and people survive it. But if you then bring that out into the political arena and recommend behavior on the basis of the merely dramatic, it's immoral.

Q. So you can manipulate your materials to fit your artwork, but if you try to carve up the world.

A. That's Fascism. Fascism is attractive in part because there is so much of the tendency to treat the world as a work of art. That wonderful section in Burckhardt on the State as a work of art is very attractive in a way . . . until you see how horrible it is.

Q. Two of the works that strike me as precursors to *The Tunnel* are *Notes from Underground* and Kafka's "The Burrow." I wonder if those are deliberate echoes in your novel.

A. Actually, I hadn't even read "The Burrow" when I started *The Tunnel*, which of course has been in progress for a long time. I read *Notes from Underground* as everybody does when he's a freshman, and I was never struck by it, although you never know how much those things percolate. Since I started the novel, of course, I've paid attention to it. But I think there's a great deal in my own background that would lead me in this direction. Then I began to pick up all the literary examples that go along with it. But I can remember back into my childhood enough about my kind of daydreams—the notions of tunnels were powerful images before much literary influence.

Q. Burrowing in, forming barriers, creating a private space that can't be penetrated by ghosts—they're presumably common psychological tactics.

A. Sure. And the ambiguity of it all denotes something common enough. I don't want it to be a "thin" notion, but I do think that the particular images that come to dominate a story have more significance for the writer than they would for the average person. Everybody has his own. And of course, there are all kinds of tunnels. Now Kafka's burrows aren't tunnels exactly, because a tunnel is presumably going from A to B in order to get *through* barriers, to get beyond obstacles, to escape. But of course, in my book, the tunnel is itself the point. You're not going anywhere.

Q. Your characters seem to lock the door only to find that they've closed themselves in with whatever they had hoped to escape from. I think of Furber trying to purge himself of his carnal urges. The purification rite is his obsession. Even though he doesn't commit the physical act. One of the saddest moments in that book is when Furber makes love with the girl by imposing his shadow upon her.

A. You can suffocate in your own fiction.

Q. We've spoken before about the relative status in reality of historical and literary figures. Would you say that Huckleberry Finn is more "real" than, say, Alexander the Great because he is more fully realized in language?

A. I certainly would. Not only that, but there are more people who lived with Huck as a real person—this may be a literary mistake, but never mind—and who see childhood, figures along the Mississippi, and the particular socio-historical milieu in the United States in this way. Frequently the novelist creates the little people of the time. I'm working with that in this book. I'm pushing it, although the novel is not simply that. I don't think the purpose of the novel is to create important nobodies who stand as significant figures for their time. But that does happen, and it isn't all bad. If one understands Tom Sawyer and Huck Finn well enough, then they are a part of the American Myth. They constitute important historical forces, and they are not divorced from all reality. Any viable myths of this sort have a grip on *something*. It's true of

Faulkner. We don't even know yet how important it's going to be, when the Faulkner characters people our historical consciousness. Dickens did that—still does for a number of people, although his effect is no longer as dominant as it was.

Q. In the *Partisan Review* interview, you said that poetry has grown careless, leaving fiction as "the advanced, hard and formal form." Would you elaborate on your disparagement of poetry? If you think of poetry, as many critics do, as the "purer" genre, it might be more conducive to the self-referentiality you seek.

A. It would normally be, and this comes out of the Symbolist movement. One would associate it with Valéry or Mallarmé. It's just that at the present moment I think that poetry is in a down phase, particularly in European literature. We passed through a phase of perhaps the greatest set of lyric poets we've had in European culture, and certainly the highest explosion of American poetic impulses. It's not unnatural that from Stevens we have lesser Lowells and Roethkes, and now we have lesser still. That I think is a temporary phenomenon. But it's also accompanied by the fact that there has been a great explosion, not of great poetry, but of poets. That hasn't helped matters. When you compare what is going on in poetry from the point of view of poetry in the larger, traditional sense, all the really fine poets now are writing fiction. I would stack up paragraphs of Hawkes, Coover, Elkin, or Gaddis against the better poets writing now. Just from the power of the poetic impulse itself, the "poets" wouldn't stand a chance.

Q. It seems, too, as though poetry, especially free verse, is so open to spontaneity in a bad sense. And in the Sixties, every performance was a work of art, and everyone was a poet, while the burden of significance was on the audience.

A. It's easier to achieve a certain kind of pseudo-identity, too, by being a poet . . . . But I don't think poetry is anywhere near the stature of fiction now. The great figures will be back, but at present we have an extraordinary period of great novels.

Q. So you're not one who worries about the continuing efficacy of the genre of the novel.

A. All you have to do is look around the world and see what's being produced, the kinds of books that are coming out, the quality they have. Whether you're reading a new novel by Calvino or Vargas Llosa—sensational writers who write quite differently—or others still, who may write nothing like Hawkes or Barth . . . it's significant stuff that's coming out, it's important. When *J R* comes out, it's a monumental effort. And that kind of thing is happening all around—stunningly good stuff. I taught some contemporary novels last year in a Philosophy and Literature course—Fuentes's *Distant Relations* and Hawkes's *Virginie* were two of the books. None of them were the major works of their authors, all were different, yet all were first-rate. Fuentes was on the campus for about a month in April, and it was exhilarating to be around him, because along with so many of his compatriots he's really revolutionizing writing. It's an exciting time.

Q. The writers that you mention most often as personal favorites—Barth, Barthelme, Coover, Elkin, Hawkes, the South American "magical realists"—are these the contemporaries who can be most directly identified with your own literary theories?

A. I would not expect, well, Fuentes to share my "hermeticism," I suppose. But when he was here—and I'm not sure why he did this—he made a point in his last lecture of referring to my views with approval maybe half a dozen times. Part of that may have been courtesy, but as I talked to him, and understanding his Leftist leanings and so forth, his conception of what one had to do as a writer was very similar to mine. I think what has happened with a lot of writers—Fuentes, who started out on the Left, realist, committed, as Calvino did—has been a shift away, a withdrawal of their radicalism, from parties. I also regard myself as a radical, but not one allied with any party. Parties force you to give up your intellect. I think we share an idea of things that need to be done, in a very general sort of way.

Q. Is it possible to accomplish what needs to be done without those affiliations?

A. I've never been called an "engaged" writer before. I don't have the deeply emotional commitment of a Márquez or a Fuentes. But both Márquez and Fuentes know that if they're going to have the social effect that they want to have, they're going to have to be artists first. Otherwise, their work won't be powerful enough, won't last long enough. It will get lost in the political climate. So they are much more susceptible to that contradiction. I felt it, of course, during the Sixties, when we were out marching and so on, but even then I had too much skepticism about all of this. Movements tend to falsify subtleties. Too often, the Sartrean idea is that we have to give this up because the end is so important, while you end up sacrificing the end as part of the means. I tend to be a Kantian about things like that. It does tend to throw you back into a position of increasing impotence. And that gets into my work. It's part of the reason why my work is as bitter as it is, I suppose. It's that sense of helplessness. You write essays on the Bomb, you go to conferences on nuclear holocaust—people think of me as a Holocaust Expert now—and you get weary of that side of it. You have to be careful not to let the exasperation poison things. Perhaps I can get rid of it in a character.

Q. You teach, or have taught, a course in Philosophy and Literature. Do you find that they work together easily, that they're compatible in the classroom?

A. I use it to teach points of view that I don't share. Philosophy *in* literature is largely content analysis. But I find it fun to treat novels on the premise that they are constructing worlds, and that you can then ask what the philosophy of those worlds are—the same way that you would ask it about *the* world—and see what goes on in the system to convey it. The structure, the plot.

Q. Do you teach your own work?

A. No.

Q. If you were required to teach your own work, would you approach it as a diligent New Critic, so as to do the most justice to the language artifact? What method do you feel would show the fullest appreciation of what you try to accomplish in your work?

A. I'm not sure. I think what you would have to do with my work, because of the attitudes behind it, is to pretend you were reading Montaigne. It's basically skeptical and non-committed, so behind it are plenty of attitudes and values that are absolute, but in terms of the theoretical frame around them, they are held with a great deal of skepticism. I'd probably be inclined to do a New Critical approach because that's the way I was brought up, although that's not what I do in the class much. Mine is generally a philosophy class more than a literature class.

Q. I wonder how you react to Post-Structuralist and other recent brands of criticism that assert themselves as works of art, rather than as something which is just occasioned by a work of art and is therefore of a second order of creation.

A. Well, I think that is very interesting. It's been done in the past, and it can work, but the question is whether or not it is written well enough. I don't think most of it is. What you have is a clear move on the part of the critic to usurp part of the creative function *for* the critic. I have no objection to that. I understand it perfectly. I do it myself. But I wouldn't make it a critical premise. A lot of it is very interesting, but a lot of it cops out, attempting to earn for the critic a creative status on other bases than creativity. Generally, this critic is doing openly what critics have done for a long time covertly. Also, this type of critic wants to make the text malleable to his own manipulations, and that's just the opposite of what my aim is when I'm creating a text. I want a text to have levels and rich-ness, but I want *it* to have that. My attitude toward the reader is one of creative passivity. When that critic approaches a text, he says that the reader is now in charge, in the sense that the text is raw material. What I believe is that when I'm reading, say Colette, the text doesn't become *me*. That's not what I'm reading her for. I want to become Colette.

Q. Is that the most beneficial way of approaching a text? Joyce always talked about creating an ideal relationship. And in *Willie Masters' Lonesome Wife*, if Babs is language herself, as lovers of language we are depicted as dilettantish, impatient, and not particularly skilled. Do you hope to create a readership by foisting demanding works upon them? In other words, do I learn how to read a Gass work by reading enough of Gass to become "schooled" effectively?

A. It is a process of schooling. It is a process, too, of giving yourself to the work. The problem is that of removing yourself to the extent that you allow the work to interpenetrate your nature, your consciousness, rather than the other way around. If you don't have this point of view, then you cease to be as interested in quality, because you can make something out of anything, just as the artist may see something ugly and make it beautiful when he writes it up. The critic who says, "All the better if it's not very good in itself—it's much more easily disarmed," is not interested in the central problem as I see it, and that is the quality of the literary product. He's interested in texts, not in why one text is better than another. One of the reasons is that *he* is going to confer upon the text the value that it will receive. Even if Roland Barthes is going to develop a huge, complex process of decoding, he chooses a lousy story by Balzac.

Q. It's as though the less successful work gives you more freedom to move around.

A. And also, it's often simply more illustrative of what you are talking about. That was true of early Freudianism, too, which seemed to work best on cheap romances. Eventually, of course, you get a sophisticated Freudian doctrine. The same thing with Marxists: the early Marxist stuff worked best on junk. I think Structuralists are still crude—you get some important insights, but everyone has his own little formulas which only eventually will be refined. It seems as though I've lived through many generations of formulas. When I grew up, it was all New Criticism, which sometimes was tiresome, but which did have something important to say.

Q. It's still the primary approach in literature surveys, I think. It's one way of getting students to respect the complexity of literature—proving it is accessible to formulas which are reminiscent of methods used in the sciences.

A. And the teachers foster the sense that it takes a special expertise to read literature adequately. It's one way of competing for respect these days.

Notes

1. Introduction: Wording a World

1. For a fuller discussion of the disruption of realist tendencies, see Jerome Klinkowitz, "The Death of the Death of the Novel," in *Literary Disruptions: The Making of a Post-Contemporary American Fiction* (Urbana: Univ. of Illinois Press, 1975), pp. 3-32.
2. William Gass, *On Being Blue: A Philosophical Inquiry* (Boston: David R. Godine, 1976), pp. 42-43.
3. William Gass, "Philosophy and the Form of Fiction," in *Fiction and the Figures of Life* (New York: Knopf, 1970), pp. 23-24.
4. Ronald Sukenick, "The Death of the Novel," in *The Death of the Novel and Other Stories* (New York: Dial, 1969), p. 41.
5. Iris Murdoch, "Against Dryness," quoted in Frank Kermode, "Fictions," in *The Sense of an Ending: Studies in the Theory of Fiction* (New York: Oxford Univ. Press, 1967), p. 132.
6. William Barrett, "Testimony of Modern Art," in *The Limits of Language*, ed. Walker Gibson (New York: Hill and Wang, 1962), pp. 72-73.
7. Thomas Pynchon, *V.* (New York: Bantam, 1963), p. 305.
8. Samuel Beckett, *Watt* (New York: Grove, 1959), p. 81.
9. Samuel Beckett, *Watt*, p. 199.
10. Werner Heisenberg, *Physics and Philosophy: The Revolution in Modern Science*, quoted in Elizabeth W. Bruss, *Beautiful Theories: The Spectacle of Discourse in Contemporary Criticism* (Baltimore: Johns Hopkins Univ. Press, 1982), p. 15.

11. Alain Robbe-Grillet, "Nature, Humanism, Tragedy," in *For a New Novel: Essays on Fiction*, trans. Richard Howard (New York: Grove, 1965), p. 72.

12. Frank Kermode, "Literary Fiction and Reality," in *The Sense of an Ending: Studies in the Theory of Fiction* (New York: Oxford University Press, 1977), p. 132.

13. William Gass, *Willie Masters' Lonesome Wife, Triquarterly Supplement* 2 (Evanston: Northwestern Univ. Press, 1968), blue section.

14. José Ortega y Gasset, "The Dehumanization of Art," in *The Dehumanization of Art and Other Essays on Art, Culture and Literature*, trans. Helene Weyl and Willard R. Trask (Princeton: Princeton Univ. Press, 1968), p. 11.

15. William Gass, "The Concept of Character in Fiction," in *Fiction and the Figures of Life*, p. 49.

16. William Gass, "In the Heart of the Heart of the Country," in *In the Heart of the Heart of the Country and Other Stories* (New York: Harper, 1968), p. 196.

17. John Ditsky, "The Man on the Quaker Oats Box: Characteristics of Recent Experimental Fiction," *Georgia Review*, 26 (1972), 309.

18. Alain Robbe-Grillet, "On Several Obsolete Notions," in *For a New Novel*, p. 43.

19. Ronald Sukenick, from a letter quoted in Raymond Federman, "Surfiction—Four Propositions in Form of an Introduction," in *Surfiction: Fiction Now . . . and Tomorrow*, ed. Raymond Federman (Chicago: Swallow, 1975), p. 5.

20. William Gass, "The Medium of Fiction," in *Fiction and the Figures of Life*, p. 27.

21. William Gass, "The Concept of Character in Fiction," in *Fiction and the Figures of Life*, p. 49.

22. William Gass, quoted in "William Gass and John Gardner: A Debate on Fiction," *New Republic* (10 March 1979), p. 31.

23. William Gass, "Philosophy and the Form of Fiction," p. 9.

24. Vladimir Nabokov, *Lectures on Literature*, ed. Fredson Bowers (New York: Harcourt, 1980), p. 5.

25. William Gass, "In the Heart of the Heart of the Country," p. 179.

26. William Gass, "The Medium of Fiction," p. 30.

27. William Gass, "In Terms of the Toenail: Fiction and the Figures of Life," in *Fiction and the Figures of Life*, p. 58.

28. William Gass, quoted in "Donald Barthelme, William Gass, Grace Paley, Walker Percy: A Symposium on Fiction," *Shenandoah*, 27 (Winter 1976), 22.

29. Quoted in Thomas LeClair, "An Interview with William Gass," in *Anything Can Happen: Interviews with Contemporary American Novelists* (Urbana: Univ. of Illinois Press, 1983), p. 175.

30. Gerald Graff, *Literature Against Itself: Literary Ideas in Modern Society* (Chicago: Univ. of Chicago Press, 1979), pp. 35–37.

31. Gerald Graff, *Literature Against Itself*, p. 54.

32. David Lodge, "The Novelist's Medium and the Novelist's Art: Problems in Criticism," in *Language of Fiction: Essays in Criticism and Verbal Analysis* (London: Routledge & Kegan Paul, 1966), p. 47.

33. William Gass, "Carrots, Noses, Snow, Rose, Roses," in *The World Within the Word* (New York: Knopf, 1978), p. 294.

34. William Gass, "Gertrude Stein and the Geography of the Sentence," in *The World Within the Word*, p. 80.

35. Alan Wilde, "Irony in the Postmodern Age: Toward a Map of Suspensiveness," *Boundary 2*, 9 (Fall 1980), 20.

36. Northrop Frye, *Anatomy of Criticism* (Princeton: Princeton Univ. Press, 1957), pp. 73–74.

37. Richard Poirier, *The Performing Self: Compositions and Decompositions in the Language of Contemporary Life* (New York: Oxford Univ. Press, 1971), p. 87.

38. Elizabeth W. Bruss, *Beautiful Theories*, pp. 165–66.

39. Raymond Federman, *The Twofold Vibration* (Bloomington: Indiana Univ. Press, 1982), p. 63.

40. William Gass, *Omensetter's Luck* (New York: New American Library, 1966), p. 216.

41. Personal interview with William Gass, Los Angeles (27 December 1982).

42. William Gass, quoted in "William Gass and John Gardner: A Debate on Fiction," p. 23.

43. Naomi Lebowitz, *Humanism and the Absurd in the Modern Novel* (Evanston: Northwestern Univ. Press, 1971), p. 126.

44. Gilbert Sorrentino, *The Imaginative Qualities of Actual Things* (New York: Random/Pantheon, 1971).

45. William Gass, *On Being Blue*, p. 87.

46. Richard Gilman, "William H. Gass," in *The Confusion of Realms* (New York: Random/Vintage, 1969), p. 72.

47. Richard Gilman, "William H. Gass," p. 72.

48. John Hawkes, quoted in Robert Scholes, *The Fabulators* (New York: Oxford Univ. Press, 1967), p. 68.

49. Gerald Graff, *Literature Against Itself*, p. 45.

50. Robert Alter, *Partial Magic: The Novel as a Self-Conscious Genre* (Berkeley: Univ. of California Press, 1975), p. x.

51. Robert Alter, *Partial Magic*, p. 222.

52. John Barth, "Life-Story," in *Lost in the Funhouse: Fiction for Print, Tape, Live Voice* (Garden City, N.Y.: Doubleday, 1968), p. 117.

53. I borrow this phrase from "The Physicality of Words," *Time* (3 May 1968), pp. 96–97.

54. Robert Alter, "Mimesis and the Motive for Fiction," *TriQuarterly*, 42 (Spring 1978), 249.

55. Arlen J. Hansen, "The Celebration of Solipsism: A New Trend in American Fiction," *Modern Fiction Studies*, 19 (Spring 1973), 9.

56. William Gass, *Willie Masters' Lonesome Wife*, white section.

2. *Omensetter's Luck:* The Fall into Language

1. William Gass, *Omensetter's Luck* (New York: New American Library, 1966), p. 31. Subsequent quotations refer to this edition and will be noted parenthetically in the text.

2. Quoted in Tom LeClair, "An Interview with William Gass," in *Anything Can Happen: Interviews with Contemporary American Novelists* (Urbana: Univ. of Illinois Press, 1983), p. 172.

3. The phrase belongs to Richard Gilman, from "William H. Gass," in *The Confusion of Realms* (New York: Random/Vintage, 1969), p. 74.

4. Larry McCaffery, *The Metafictional Muse: The Works of Robert Coover, Donald Barthelme, and William H. Gass* (Pittsburgh: Univ. of Pittsburgh Press, 1982), p. 226.

5. Marcus Klein submits this useful term in "John Hawkes' Experimental Compositions," in *Surfiction: Fiction Now . . . and Tomorrow*, ed. Raymond Federman (Chicago: Swallow, 1975), p. 211.

6. William Gass, "Groping for Trouts," in *The World Within the Word* (New York: Knopf, 1976), pp. 262–63.

7. George Steiner, "Silence and the Poet," in *Language and Silence: Essays on Language, Literature, and the Inhuman* (New York: Atheneum, 1967), pp. 36–37.

8. Richard J. Schneider, "The Fortunate Fall in William Gass's *Omensetter's Luck*," *Critique: Studies in Modern Fiction*, 18 (Summer 1976), 12.

9. McCaffery, *The Metafictional Muse*, pp. 234–35.

10. Marcel Raymond, *From Baudelaire to Surrealism*, The Documents of Modern Art, vol. 10, trans. G. M., dir. Robert Mothewell (New York: Wittenborn, Schultz, 1949), p. 8.

11. William Gass, "The Ontology of the Sentence, or How to Make a World of Words," in *The World Within the Word*, p. 317.

12. William Gass, "Carrots, Noses, Snow, Rose, Roses," in *The World Within the Word*, p. 301.

13. Lee Thayer, "Introduction to the Series," in Winston Weathers, *The Broken Word: The Communication Pathos in Modern Literature*, Communication and the Human Condition, vol. 1, ed. Lee Thayer (New York: Gordon and Breach, 1981), p. vii.

14. McCaffery, *The Metafictional Muse*, p. 245.

15. Jeffrey L. Duncan, "A Conversation with Stanley Elkin and William Gass," *Iowa Review*, 7, no. 1 (1976), 68.

16. Elizabeth W. Bruss, *Beautiful Theories: The Spectacle of Discourse in Contemporary Criticism* (Baltimore: Johns Hopkins Univ. Press, 1982), p. 143.

17. Northrop Frye, "City of the End of Things," in *The Modern Century* (Toronto: Oxford Univ. Press, 1967), pp. 24–25.

18. William Gass, "The Doomed in Their Sinking," in *The World Within the Word*, p. 8.

19. Frye, "City of the End of Things," p. 26.
20. Schneider, "The Fortunate Fall," 17.
21. McCaffery, *The Metafictional Muse*, p. 249.
22. Robert Frost, "Mending Wall," 11. 32–33, in *The Complete Poems of Robert Frost* (New York: Holt, 1949), p. 48.
23. John Keats, "Ode to a Nightingale," 11. 73–74, in *John Keats: Selected Poems and Letters*, ed. Douglas Bush (Boston: Houghton, 1959), p. 207.
24. Schneider, "The Fortunate Fall," 18.

3. *In the Heart of the Heart of the Country:* Eyes Driven Back In

1. William Gass, "The Pedersen Kid," in *In the Heart of the Heart of the Country and Other Stories* (New York: Harper, 1968), p. 1. Subsequent quotations refer to this edition and will be noted parenthetically in the text.
2. Bruce Bassoff neatly provides the foundations for these various readings in "The Sacrificial World of William Gass: *In the Heart of the Heart of the Country*," *Critique: Studies in Modern Fiction*, 18 (August 1976), 36–42.
3. Larry McCaffery, *The Metafictional Muse: The Works of Robert Coover, Donald Barthelme, and William H. Gass* (Pittsburgh: Univ. of Pittsburgh Press, 1982), p. 187.
4. William Gass, "Preface" to *In the Heart of the Heart of the Country* (New York: Pocket Books, 1977), p. 18.
5. Patricia Kane advances this theory in "The Sun Burned on the Snow: Gass's 'The Pedersen Kid,'" *Critique: Studies in Modern Fiction*, 14 (Fall 1972), 90.
6. William Gass, "Imaginary Borges and His Books," in *Fiction and the Figures of Life* (New York: Knopf, 1970), p. 131.
7. William Gass, "Mrs. Mean," in *In the Heart of the Heart of the Country* (New York: Harper, 1968), p. 8. Subsequent quotations will be noted parenthetically in the text.
8. William Gass, "The Leading Edge of the Trash Phenomenon," in *Fiction and the Figures of Life*, p. 98.

9. Larry McCaffery, who focuses at length on the theme of sexual preoccupation in "Mrs. Mean," makes the point that the narrator's desire to "penetrate" the walls of the woman's dark house is an extension of his sexual curiosity, in *The Metafictional Muse*, p. 200.

10. Nabokov's Humbert Humbert epitomizes the ultimate insufficiency of the verbal surrogate. Humbert memorably proposes that words have a sensual delectability of their own: "Lolita, light of my life, fire of my loins. My sin, my soul. Lo-lee-ta: the tip of the tongue taking a trip of three steps down the palate to tap at three, on the teeth. Lo. Lee. Ta." Vladimir Nabokov, *Lolita* (New York: Putnam, 1955), p. 11. Nevertheless, Humbert does not abstain from more immediate contact with his beloved.

11. William Gass, "Icicles," in *In the Heart of the Heart of the Country* (New York: Harper, 1968), pp. 111–12. Subsequent quotations will be noted parenthetically in the text.

12. T. S. Eliot, "Gerontion," in *The Complete Poems and Plays: 1909–1950* (New York: Harcourt, 1971), pp. 21, 1, 16.

13. Larry McCaffery expands upon Pearson's name to suggest that it includes the ironic possibilities of "person" and "peer," both of which are inappropriate to this utterly self-centered, dehumanizing individual. See *The Metafictional Muse*, p. 204.

14. William Gass, "Philosophy and the Form of Fiction," in *Fiction and the Figures of Life*, p. 6.

15. William Gass, "Philosophy and the Form of Fiction," p. 7.

16. William Gass, "The Ontology of the Sentence," in *The World Within the Word* (New York: Knopf, 1978), p. 317.

17. William Gass, *On Being Blue: A Philosophical Inquiry* (Boston: David R. Godine, 1976), p. 30.

18. William Gass, "Preface" to *In the Heart of the Heart of the Country* (New York: Pocket Books, 1977), p. 25.

19. Charles Russell, "Individual Voice in the Collective Discourse: Literary Innovation in Postmodern American Fiction," *Sub-stance*, 27 (1980), 31.

20. José Ortega y Gasset, "The Dehumanization of Art," in *The Dehumanization of Art and Other Essays on Art, Culture and Litera-*

ture, trans. Helene Weyl and Willard R. Trask (Princeton: Princeton Univ. Press, 1968), p. 36.

21. William Gass, "The Order of Insects," in *In the Heart of the Heart of the Country* (New York: Harper, 1968), p. 164. Subsequent quotations will be noted parenthetically in the text.

22. Eusebio L. Rodriguez mentions the "kinship" between the woman and Pimber in "A Nymph at Her Orisons: An Analysis of William Gass's 'Order of Insects,'" *Studies in Short Fiction*, 17 (Summer 1980), 350.

23. William Gass, "A Letter to the Editor," in *Afterwords: Novelists on Their Novels*, ed. Thomas McCormack (New York: Harper, 1969), p. 93.

24. William Gass, quoted in "Donald Barthelme, William Gass, Grace Paley, Walker Percy: A Symposium on Fiction," *Shenandoah*, 27 (Winter 1976), 7.

25. William Gass, "In the Heart of the Heart of the Country," in *In the Heart of the Heart of the Country* (New York: Harper, 1968), p. 173. Subsequent quotations will be noted parenthetically in the text.

26. William Gass, "Wisconsin Death Trip," in *The World Within the Word*, p. 41.

27. Frederick Busch, "But This Is What It Is to Live in Hell: William Gass's 'In the Heart of the Heart of the Country,'" *Modern Fiction Studies*, 20 (Autumn 1974), 99.

28. Ronald Sukenick, "Thirteen Digressions," *Partisan Review*, 43, no. 1 (1976), 99–100.

29. William Gass, "In Terms of the Toenail: Fiction and the Figures of Life," in *Fiction and the Figures of Life*, p. 71.

30. William Gass, "Groping for Trouts," in *The World Within the Word*," p. 266.

31. William Gass, "Gertrude Stein: Her Escape from Protective Language," in *Fiction and the Figures of Life*, p. 89.

32. Tony Tanner, *City of Words: American Fiction 1950–1970* (New York: Harper, 1971), p. 270.

33. William Gass, "Carrots, Noses, Snow, Rose, Roses," in *The World Within the Word*, p. 282.

34. Ronald Sukenick, quoted in Jerome Klinkowitz, "Literary Disruptions: Or, What's Become of American Fiction," in *Sur-*

fiction: Fiction Now . . . and Tomorrow, ed. Raymond Federman (Chicago: Swallow, 1975), p. 178.

35. McCaffery, *The Metafictional Muse*, pp. 219–20.

4. Willie Masters' Lonesome Wife: The Flesh Made Word

1. Leo Marx, *The Machine in the Garden: Technology and the Pastoral Ideal in America* (New York: Oxford Univ. Press, 1964), pp. 22–23.
2. Robert Frost, "The Figure a Poem Makes," quoted in Marx, *The Machine in the Garden*, p. 30.
3. Frederick R. Karl, *American Fictions, 1940–1980: A Comprehensive History and Critical Evaluation* (New York: Harper, 1983), p. 41.
4. William Gass, *Willie Masters' Lonesome Wife*, *TriQuarterly Supplement* 2 (Evanston: Northwestern Univ. Press, 1968), olive section. The novella is nonpaginated and divided into four sections: blue, olive, red, and white. Subsequent quotations will be noted in the text according to section color.
5. Michel Foucault, *The Order of Things: An Archaeology of the Human Sciences*, trans. anon. (New York: Random, 1970; Vintage, 1973), p. 49.
6. Gertrude Stein, quoted by Thornton Wilder, in his "Introduction" to *Four in America* (New Haven: Yale Univ. Press, 1947), pp. v–vi.
7. Gertrude Stein, quoted by Thornton Wilder in his "Introduction" to *Four in America*, p. vi.
8. William Gass, *On Being Blue: A Philosophical Inquiry* (Boston: David R. Godine, 1976), p. 32.
9. Gass, *On Being Blue*, p. 17.
10. Gass, *On Being Blue*, pp. 57–58.
11. Reed B. Merrill, "The Grotesque as Structure: *Willie Masters' Lonesome Wife*," *Criticism*, 18 (Fall 1976), 309.
12. Donald Barthelme, *Snow White* (New York: Atheneum, 1967), p. 6.
13. Charles Caramello, "Fleshing Out *Willie Masters' Lonesome Wife*," *Sub-stance*, 27 (1980), 60.

14. William Gass, quoted in "Pole-Vaulting in Top Hats: A Public Conversation with John Barth, William Gass, and Ishmael Reed," *Modern Fiction Studies*, 22 (Summer 1976), 147.
15. William Gass, "The Artist and Society," in *Fiction and the Figures of Life* (New York: Knopf, 1970), p. 287.
16. William Gass, "Philosophy and the Form of Fiction," in *Fiction and the Figures of Life*, p. 13.
17. William Gass, "The Medium of Fiction," in *Fiction and the Figures of Life*, p. 27.
18. This particular effect is only achieved in the original *TriQuarterly Supplement* 2. The reprinted edition of the novella (Knopf, 1971) homogenizes the text.
19. As expected, not every critic is so enamored of Gass's inventiveness. Denis Donoghue suggests that Gass provides an arbitrary festival which is too eager to sell out profundity in favor of sheer exhibitionism: "The reader may or may not take pleasure in the spectacle of traditionally rich resources of wisdom smilingly disowned." See *Ferocious Alphabets* (Boston: Little, Brown, 1981), p. 89.
20. For a detailed analysis of the "spatial novel," see Sharon Spencer, *Space, Time and Structure in the Modern Novel* (New York: New York Univ. Press, 1971).
21. James Phelan, *Worlds from Words: A Theory of Language in Fiction* (Chicago: Univ. of Chicago Press, 1981), p. 214.

5. *The Tunnel:* Recent Excavations

1. Gass offers these theoretical guidelines in his interview with Tom LeClair, in *Anything Can Happen: Interviews with Contemporary American Novelists* (Urbana: Univ. of Illinois Press, 1983), p. 171.
2. Quoted in Bradford Morrow, "An Interview with William Gass," *Conjunctions*, 4 (Spring-Summer 1983), 15.
3. William Gass, "Why Windows Are Important to Me," *TriQuarterly*, 20 (Winter 1971), 295. Subsequent quotations will be noted parenthetically as "Why Windows" in the text.

4. William Gass, "Koh Whistles Up a Wind," *TriQuarterly*, 41 (Fall 1977), 203. Subsequent quotations will be noted parenthetically as "Koh Whistles" in the text.

5. Quoted in Bradford Morrow, "An Interview with William Gass," 16.

6. William Gass, "Life in a Chair," *Salmagundi*, 55 (Winter 1982), 18. Subsequent quotations will be noted parenthetically as "Life in a Chair" in the text.

7. William Gass, "The Cost of Everything," *Fiction*, 1, no. 3 (1972), nonpaginated. Subsequent quotations will be noted parenthetically as "The Cost of Everything" in the text.

8. William Gass, "Mad Meg," *Iowa Review*, 7 (Winter 1976), 78. Subsequent quotations will be noted parenthetically as "Mad Meg" in the text.

9. Samuel Beckett, *Murphy* (New York: Grove, 1957).

10. William Gass, "Uncle Balt and the Nature of Being," *Conjunctions*, 2 (Spring–Summer 1982), 25–26. Subsequent quotations will be noted parenthetically as "Uncle Balt" in the text.

11. George Steiner admonishes us to keep clearly in mind the fact that the German language itself retains the taint of the Nazi horrors, so that one is the captive of a contaminated medium. As he so vividly puts it:

It is not merely that a Hitler, a Goebbels, and a Himmler happened to speak German. Nazism found in the language precisely what it needed to give voice to its savagery. Hitler heard inside his native tongue the latent hysteria, the confusion, the quality of hypnotic trance. He plunged unerringly into the undergrowth of language, into those zones of darkness and outcry which are the infancy of articulate speech, and which come before words have grown mellow and provisional to the touch of the mind. He sensed in German another music than that of Goethe, Heine, and Mann; a rasping cadence, half nebulous jargon, half obscenity. And instead of turning away in nauseated disbelief, the German people gave massive echo to the man's bellowing. It bellowed back out of a million throats and smashed-down boots.

See "The Hollow Miracle," in *Language and Silence: Essays on Language, Literature, and the Inhuman* (New York: Atheneum, 1967), p. 99.

12. William Gass, "Susu, I approach you in my dreams," *TriQuarterly*, 42 (Spring 1978), 132. Subsequent quotations will be noted parenthetically as "Susu" in the text.

13. Richard L. Rubenstein offers a provocative analysis of both the roots and the continuing evidence of our propensity for institutionalizing inhumanity in *The Cunning of History: The Holocaust and the American Future* (New York: Harper, 1975). Of specific relevance are his opening chapters, "Mass Death and Contemporary Civilization" and "Bureaucratic Domination."

14. George Steiner, "Humane Literacy," in *Language and Silence*, p. 5.

15. Quoted in Tom LeClair, "An Interview with William Gass," p. 170.

16. George Steiner, "The Retreat from the Word," in *Language and Silence*, p. 25.

17. William Gass, "We Have Not Lived the Right Life," *New American Review*, no. 5 (1969), 24. Subsequent quotations will be noted parenthetically as "We Have Not Lived" in the text.

18. William Gass, "Summer Bees," *Paris Review*, 79 (1981), 233.

19. William Gass, "The Old Folks," *Kenyon Review*, 1 (Winter 1979), 38. Subsequent quotations will be noted parenthetically as "Old Folks" in the text.

20. Frank Kermode, "Fictions," in *The Sense of an Ending: Studies in the Theory of Fiction* (New York: Oxford Univ. Press, 1967), p. 39.

21. Quoted in Tom LeClair, "An Interview with William Gass," p. 170.

22. William Gass, "The Artist and Society," in *Fiction and the Figures of Life* (New York: Knopf, 1970), pp. 283–84.

6. The Aesthetic of Doubt in Recent Fiction

1. See, for example, "A Writers' Forum on Moral Fiction," *Fiction International*, 2/3, no. 12 (1980), 5–25.

2. John Gardner, *On Moral Fiction* (New York: Basic Books, 1977), p. 9.

3. Gardner, *On Moral Fiction*, p. 6.

4. Gardner, *On Moral Fiction*, p. 16.

5. "William Gass and John Gardner: A Debate on Fiction," *New Republic* (10 March 1979), p. 28.

6. Quoted by Stephen Singular, in "The Sound and Fury Over Fiction," *The New York Times Magazine* (8 July 1979), p. 15.

7. "William Gass and John Gardner: A Debate on Fiction," p. 28.

8. This point is argued at length by Jerome Klinkowitz in "The Effacement of Contemporary American Literature," *College English*, 42 (1980), 382–89.

9. Myron Greenman, "Understanding New Fiction," *Modern Fiction Studies*, 20 (Autumn 1974), 315.

10. Ronald Sukenick, "Twelve Digressions Toward a Study of Composition," *New Literary History*, 6 (1975), 429.

11. Sukenick, "Twelve Digressions," 431.

12. Austin Warren, "The Nature and Modes of Narrative," in *Theory of Literature* (New York: Harcourt, 1949), p. 220.

13. Sukenick, "Twelve Digressions," 436–37.

14. Bernard Bergonzi, *The Situation of the Novel* (London: Macmillan, 1970; rpt. Pittsburgh: Univ. of Pittsburgh Press, 1970), p. 19. Bergonzi recognizes the dilemma of the contemporary novelist, who has inherited the urge to innovate, but who finds himself at a point (post-Proust, post-Joyce) where the novel may have finished off its possibilities. He suggests that the continued vitality of the novel will require new critical procedures to cope with its new challenges.

15. See, for example, John Barth, "The Literature of Replenishment," *Atlantic* (January 1980), pp. 65–71; also see Jerome Klinkowitz, *Literary Disruptions: The Making of a Post-Contemporary American Fiction*, 2d ed. (Urbana: Univ. of Illinois Press, 1980). Both argue that recent works of experimental fiction powerfully show that the novel is in an age of unusual prosperity.

16. Richard Poirier, *The Performing Self* (New York: Oxford Univ. Press, 1971), pp. 3–4.

17. Ronald Sukenick, "Innovative Fiction/Innovative Criteria: Ronald Sukenick on Reinventing the Novel," *Fiction International*, 2/3 (Spring/Fall 1976), 134.

18. Leo Tolstoy, *War and Peace*, trans. Louise and Aylmer Maude, ed. George Gibian (New York: Norton, 1966), pp. 301–2.

19. Kurt Vonnegut, *Slaughterhouse-Five; or, The Children's Crusade* (New York: Delacorte/Seymour Lawrence, 1969), pp. 185–86.

20. Iris Murdoch, "Against Dryness: A Polemical Sketch," in *The Novel Today: Contemporary Writers on Modern Fiction*, ed. Malcolm Bradbury (Manchester, England: Manchester Univ. Press, 1977), p. 29. Murdoch goes on to warn against posing facile consolations of conventional fictional form now that more substantial concepts of truth are absent.

21. Larry McCaffery, "The Gass-Gardner Debate: Showdown on Main Street," *Literary Review*, 23 (Fall 1979), 139.

22. Tolstoy, *War and Peace*, pp. 737–39.

23. E. L. Doctorow, *The Book of Daniel* (New York: Random, 1971), pp. 42–43.

24. Quoted by Deirdre Bair, in *Samuel Beckett: A Biography* (New York: Harcourt, 1978; rpt. New York: Harvest, 1980), p. 640.

25. Philip Stevick, *Alternative Pleasures: Postrealist Fiction and the Tradition* (Urbana: Univ. of Illinois Press, 1981), p. 37.

26. Warner Berthoff, *A Literature Without Qualities: American Writing Since 1945* (Berkeley: Univ. of California Press, 1979).

27. Susan Sontag, "Against Interpretation," in *Against Interpretation and Other Essays* (New York: Dell/Delta, 1961), p. 24.

28. Sontag, "Against Interpretation," p. 25.

29. Raymond Federman, *Take It or Leave It* (New York: Fiction Collective, 1976), n. p.

30. Roland Barthes, *The Pleasure of the Text*, quoted by Raymond Federman, in "What Are Experimental Novels and Why Are There So Many Left Unread?" *Genre*, 14 (Spring 1981), 28.

31. Federman, "What Are Experimental Novels," 30.

32. Annie Dilliard, *Living By Fiction* (New York: Harper, 1982), p. 28.

33. Charles Russell, "The Vault of Language: Self-Reflective Artifice in Contemporary American Fiction," *Modern Fiction Studies*, 20 (1974), 359.

Index

DATE DUE

PRINTED IN U.S.A.